Design
Sourcebook

MOSAICS

Design
Sourcebook

MOSAICS

MARTIN CHEEK

NEW HOLLAND

CONTENTS

INTRODUCTION

THE APPEAL OF MOSAIC has rocketed in recent years. This ancient art is now enjoying a renaissance and mosaic artists are once more finding themselves working in close conjunction with architects and interior designers.

Thanks to the many home-style publications and popular television programmes, the public, too, now realize that it is possible to commission wonderful mosaics for their own home. But where do you start? Who do you choose and how do you contact an artist whose work you like?

Design Sourcebook Mosaics has the answer to these questions. With its atttractive design, wonderful, full-colour images and featuring the work of more than 40 artists, it provides a unique directory of contemporary work.

The book has been arranged into subjects for ease of reference. Starting with the natural world, through the human world, abstract designs, still life and mosaic as sculpture, it also includes a special

section on pebble mosaic featuring the stunning work of Maggy Howarth.

Design Sourcebook Mosaics provides inspirational signposts from the professionals. Although it is true to say that every artist learns from his or

her own mistakes, it is also possible to learn by studying examples of great

contemporary work.

It is not only beginners who sometimes experience the artist's equivalent of "writer's block".

Even the most experienced artist will occasionally feel stuck in a rut, or

temporarily run out of new ideas. With its diverse subject matter and styles, this

book cannot fail to rekindle flagging imagination. And by showing the same subject

tackled in different ways, it offers great stimulus for anyone trying to finalize the

design ideas for their next mosaic.

An individual artist's style develops naturally over the years. As a portfolio of work is built up,

certain personal traits begin to emerge. Eventually, the keen eye will be able to recognize the work of

specific artists. This is of great interest and benefit to non-professionals struggling to make their voice

heard above the throng of the mediocre.

Above all, this book is dedicated to the thousands of artists who, over the centuries, have made

wonderful mosaics, and it was created in the happy realization that thousands more artists will

continue to do so in the future.

Martin Cheek

MARTIN CHEEK

THE NATURAL WORLD

THE NATURAL WORLD IS all around us: Wonderful and unexpected colour combinations, violence and serenity, war and peace. Included here are mosaics that celebrate Nature's own unique way of problem solving:

how to propagate, hunt or avoid being eaten. The intricate forms of a conculvus attract bees to pollinate (p. 64) and the astonishing markings of a tiger camouflage it in its natural habitat (p. 46). Artists have always drawn inspiration from the wonders of nature, and mosaicists are no exception.

◭ **Ammonite** (detail). Catherine Parkinson. Marble. 7 ½ in (19 cm) square. 1996

We know about the first plants and the earliest animals from fossils, so it seems entirely fitting to open this section with this textural piece, executed with subtle, natural colours.

◭ **Otter.** Martin Cheek. Detail from Taliesin Mosaic (p. 43).

◗ **Tree of Life.** Raymond Gordon. Vitreous glass, unglazed ceramic and smalti. 48 x 36 in (120 x 90 cm). 1996

This single image sums up the whole natural world. Birds and animals, at the same time both symbolic and exotic, are depicted here together in serene harmony on and around a vast tree of life-giving potency.

MARINE LIFE

The underwater world is full of vivid colours and dynamic

shapes, so to try and capture the effect of fish and other sea

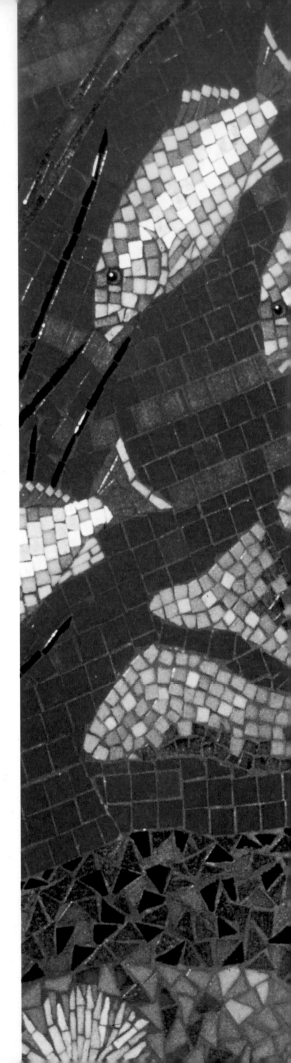

creatures swimming through water presents a great

challenge for the mosaic artist. The reason why fish

make such a good subject for a mosaic is simple: with

their fishy scales, they look like a mosaic already! By

considering the "line of action" of a subject and

continuing that line through into the background, its

movement (*andamento*) can be emphasized. By changing that

line slightly, making it thicker in parts or thinner in others,

waves can be created whose rhythms suggest ripples running

across the water.

◖ **Sea horse.** Jeni Stewart-Smith. Vitreous glass, unglazed ceramic and stained glass.
10 x 5 in (25 x 12.5 cm). 1997

*A happy, graphically stylized design. The bold curves and feminine delicacy of sea
horses make them an ever-popular choice for mosaic artists.*

◗ **Under the Sea.** Tessa Hunkin/Mosaic Workshop. Vitreous glass.
26 sq yards (26 sq m). 1993

*Even the strong, vibrant blue of the sea cannot overwhelm the glorious colours of the
fish and weed in this mosaic. The sense of depth and of being underwater is a
spectacular achievement.*

Goldfish Mirror. Tessa Hunkin/Mosaic Workshop. Vitreous glass. 47 x 24 in (120 x 60 cm). 1993

The shape and placement of the fish are perfect for this elliptical-shaped mirror and the vividly coloured fish stand out well against a deep, rich blue background without loss of definition. Such flowing compositions only work where there are no corners to break the natural flow.

John Dory. Martin Cheek. Smalti and mirror. 37 ½ x 25 ½ in (95 x 65 cm). 1997

My aim here was to try to capture the feeling of the fish moving through water in a realistic way. The opus of the blue background is intentionally "crazy", to suggest the movement of the water as the John Dory passes through it. The reeds running in front and behind help to give the composition a sense of space, and by planting them in the sea bed, a simple landscape is created.

John Dory. Peter Massey. Vitreous glass, unglazed ceramic and gold. 19 x 18 in (49 x 46 cm). 1996

Three of the colours used for the body of this fish - white, cream and golden ochre - are mosaiced in unglazed ceramic, whose non-reflective quality visually pushes back, allowing the vitreous glass highlights to come forward by contrast.

Two Mackerel. Martin Cheek. Vitreous glass. 39 x 16 in (100 x 40 cm). 1996

These fish were drawn from life and each time I glanced at them, they appeared to change colour - the pattern changing from blue or purple to turquoise and green. Mosaic is the perfect medium to use when creating fish because it, too, reacts differently to changing light. Metallic-veined tiles are ideal to describe the wonderful iridescence of these splendid sea creatures.

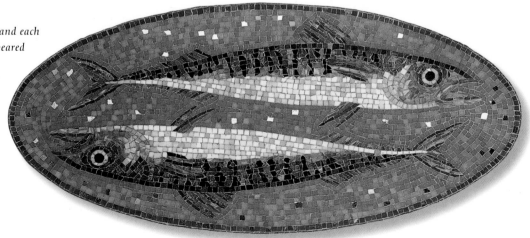

Fish panel (details below left and right). Tessa Hunkin/Mosaic Workshop.

Placing complementary colours (those which appear opposite each other on the colour wheel) such as this vibrant orange fish in strong blue water, will ensure that the subject stands out well against its surroundings. The stylization of both this fish, and the one below, couldn't be simpler or more effective.

Fish table top. Joanna Dewfall. Unglazed ceramic. 18 x 24 in (46 x 61 cm). 1990

This fantastic creature looks more like an X-ray of a fish than a real one. The surrounding sea horses, starfish and shells are handled in a symbolic rather than realistic way. Limiting the palette to eight or nine colours, as here, provides uniformity.

These fish are mosaiced in clear, bright colours so they zing out at you. But the background is equally strong, one can feel the layers of depth as the eye travels down the image. The large, deep red fish at the bottom provides the necessary "weight" to support the rest of the mosaic. Large shoals are suggested by "cutting off" the fish at the edge of the piece.

15

MARINE LIFE

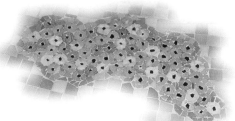

Halewell Swimming Pool
(pages 16-18). Martin Cheek and Sylvia Bell.
Vitreous glass. 1995

This was my first swimming pool commission and it was slightly daunting.

Since the cost of making designs to cover the whole pool proved prohibitive, we came up with the idea of these individual motifs. Frogs, newts and fish were surrounded by the standard Pacific blend of pool tiles which comes in three shades of blue. I first mosaiced each subject on stretched paper. Then the *opus vermiculatum* was added, taking care to place the palest blue next to the dark areas, and vice versa. Strips of Pacific blend were then placed as near as possible to the mosaic, making sure that the horizontal and vertical grids were square. Finally, individual tiles were nibbled to fill the remaining gaps.

Metamorphosis of the Frog.

As you enter the pool, the life-cycle of the frog welcomes you down each successive step, beginning with frog spawn at the top, then tadpoles, through to froglets and finally, at the bottom, a fully-grown frog. Elsewhere on the sides of the pool there are other frogs swimming towards you, diving into the water and generally having fun.

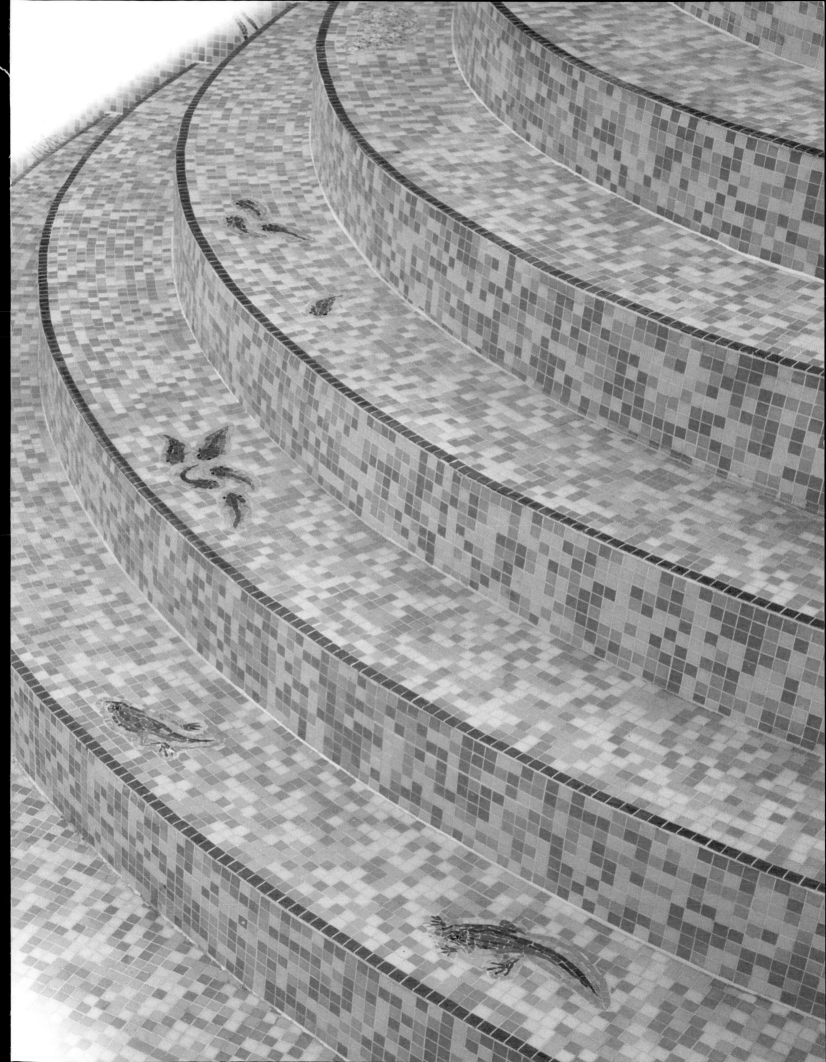

Leaping Brown Trout (details from Halewell Swimming Pool). Martin Cheek.

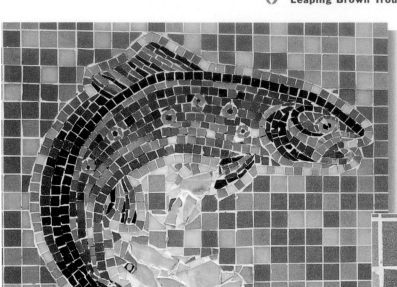

This trout is one of five that make up an animated sequence of movement, showing the fish leaping along the side of the pool wall. The broken, "crazily" worked mirror creates the splashing water effect. Using long, thin tesserae for the fins gives a more delicate look and differentiates them from the more solid pieces that make up the body of the fish.

Crayfish (detail from Halewell Swimming Pool). Sylvia Bell.

To try and simplify this complicated, highly engineered, intricate creature in terms of mosaic tesserae was a technical challenge in itself. The opus vermiculatum does an important job here, neatly cleaning up the spiky legs and claws ready to meet the background.

⊳ Fish tile.

Jeni Stewart-Smith. Vitreous glass, stained glass, unglazed ceramic and leaded edging. 8 in (20.5 cm) square. 1995

The use of a lead strip to describe the sweeping curve of the backbone of this beautifully drawn fish provides a strong contrast to the uniformity of the background tiles.

⬡ Fishmongers (detail). Kenneth Budd. Smalti and glazed ceramic. Overall size: 72 x 48 in (180 x 120 cm). 1990

The bold, graphic style of the father and son team, Kenneth and Oliver Budd, is perfectly suited to the medium of mosaic. This work was one of seven public pieces commissioned to liven up a pedestrian subway.

⬡ Harlequin Fish. Anne Heathman. Vitreous glass and raku-fired tile. 18 ¾ x 10 ¾ in (43 x 27 cm). 1997

I love the harlequin pattern on the back of the fish, as well as his stripey head and fins. The choice of colours is as unusual as it is inspired. This was Anne's first attempt at mosaic.

Sea Horse. Liz Simms. Vitreous glass and smalti. 6 ½ x 4 ⅝ in (16.5 x 11.5 cm). 1996

Often, the smaller the mosaic, the harder it is to make it work. This one is a little gem - the character of the sea horse is particularly well observed. The fact that the subject is created in rich yellow and brown smalti helps enormously, enabling it to stand proud of the thinner vitreous sea behind.

Yellow-edged Lyretail Sea Bass. Martin Cheek. Vitreous glass, mirror, gold and silver smalti. 33 x 16 in (84 x 41 cm). 1993

Here is an example of the material suggesting the subject. My motivation behind making this piece was based purely on a desire to use a lot of red, which I had hitherto never managed.

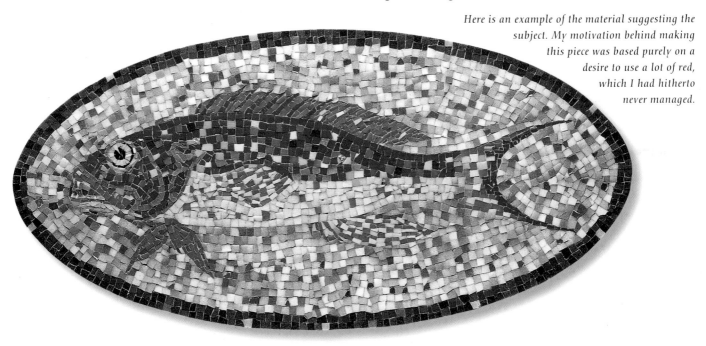

Yellow Grouper. Mark Holihan. Vitreous glass. 11 ¾ x 17 ⅜ in (29.5 x 43.5 cm). 1996

This fish is taken from a 19th-century, hand-coloured lithograph by Francis Day which appeared in his book The Fishes of Malabar. Mark uses the strong yellows and black in the marking to describe the form. The surrounding blues, though busy, work because of their contrast with the fish.

▷ **Turtle.** Liz Simms. Vitreous tile, smalti and mirror. 16 ¾ x 24 ⅜ in (42 x 61 cm). 1994

This mosaic was made in the direct method, so the smalti shell of the turtle stands proud of the vitreous sea by about ⅜ in (1 cm). There is a keen sense of the turtle's slow progress through the water, which has been achieved by making the ripples fat and undulating .

△ **Fish No.1.**
Susan Goldblatt. Vitreous glass. 20 x 18 in (51 x 46 cm). 1995

The andamento of this piece is a dynamic forward thrust led by the fish head. As this brightly rendered denizen of the deep spearheads its way through the water, one can really feel the movement which is handled in a way reminiscent of sparks flying off fireworks.

Batfish. Martin Cheek. Smalti and mirror. 37 x 25 ½ in (95 x 65 cm). 1997

I came across this obscure, surreal-looking Indo-Pacific fish in a book of lithographs. I also liked his grotesque character and relished the novelty of mosaicing all that blue, stripy, fishy flesh.

Octopus (detail). Emma Biggs/Mosaic Workshop. Vitreous glass. 39 x 20 in (100 x 50 cm). 1993

There is a strong, graphic sense of pattern on the skin of this lively octopus. The feeling of the writhing, twirling and untwirling movement of all those rubbery legs works especially well.

Resting Plaice. Martin Cheek. Unglazed ceramic and vitreous glass. 12 x 8 ½ in (30 x 22 cm). 1996

Here the natural patina of the background ceramic tiles is a gift, adding a "sandy" quality to the piece. The caramel glass tesserae "peppering" the background were added to echo the shiny orange spots of the plaice.

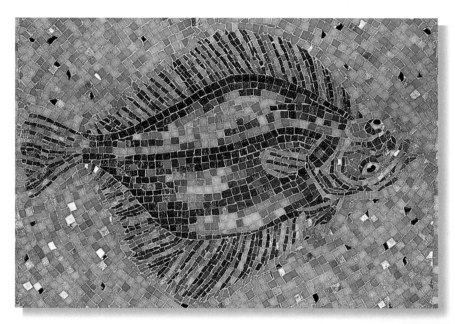

Swimming Plaice. Martin Cheek. Vitreous glass. 22 x 14 in (56 x 36 cm). 1994

In contrast to the turbot below, my aim here was to try and show the large range of colours and tones visible on these flat fish as they swim along.

Turbot. Martin Cheek. Vitreous glass, silver smalti and mirror. 31 ½ x 23 ½ in (80 x 60 cm). 1995

I love the dominant, flat presence of turbot and wanted to see if I could reproduce it in mosaic. Large areas of mosaic - such as this fish's body - will not appear uninteresting so long as there is good texture and movement, or andamento, within it.

Emperor Angel Fish. Martin Cheek. Vitreous glass.
15 ½ x 8 in (40 x 20 cm). 1997

*Small, brightly coloured tropical fish such as this one
can have intricate markings. The emperor's clean blue
and yellow stripes have a bold and very graphic feel
and are a gift to mosaic artists. The actual shape
of this fish is equally distinctive and I cut out this
mosaic to make a free-standing plaque to
emphasize its graphic quality.*

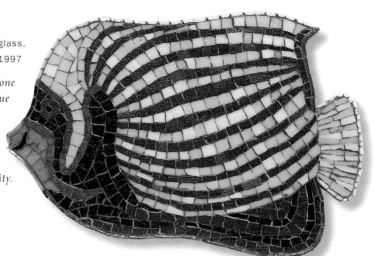

Black Widow Angel Fish. Martin Cheek.
Vitreous glass. 24 x 18 ½ in (61 x 47 cm). 1996

*In real life, this fish is tiny, only measuring about
1 ¼ in (3 cm) long. Even though my version was
greatly enlarged, I still had some difficulty in
managing to include all of the colours on its gaily
painted body.*

25

MARINE LIFE

Threadfin Angel Fish.
Martin Cheek. Vitreous glass.
22 ½ x 14 ½ in (58 x 37 cm).
1997

*This piece was made as a
paving slab using the indirect
method. The subtle variation
in the pastel shades that
smalti offers (the basic range
is 96 colours as opposed to 48
for vitreous) made it an ideal
choice for the delicate body of
this tropical fish.*

Blue Tang in Green Sea. Elizabeth Raybee. Unglazed ceramic. 47 in (120 cm) square. 1991

*Elizabeth Raybee is a mosaic artist whose work is so strong and vigorous that we felt that her
pieces need to be seen on their own. An unusual combination of
fish, starfish and anemones is wonderfully realized in this piece.
I particularly like the delicacy of the anemone's feathery fronds.
Compare the calm background of the sea bed with the dynamic,
whirling movement of the water above.*

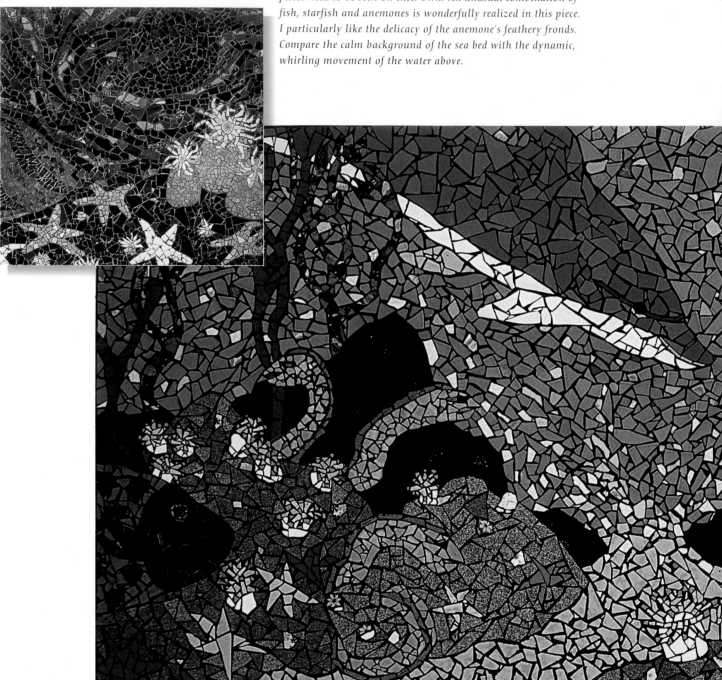

Pacific Scenes. Elizabeth Raybee. Unglazed ceramic. 94 ½ x 41 ½ in (240 x 105 cm). 1993

This large mosaic mural is an excellent example of Raybee's work - there is a true sense of being under the water. The tranquillity of this scene is disturbed by the ominous presence of the shark and moray eels. I love the way the red and orange starfish zing out of the picture.

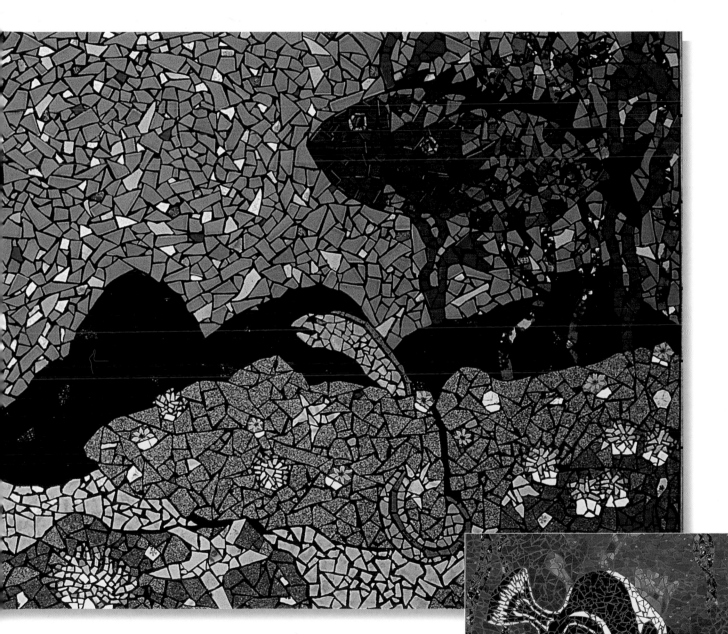

Angel in the Weeds. Elizabeth Raybee. Unglazed ceramic. 47 in (120 cm) square. 1991

Few mosaics are much more striking than this vibrant piece. Notice how the background colours all have a similar tone so as not to detract from the weight of the angel fish.

BIRDS

The vibrantly coloured, spiky plumage of many

birds is a great challenge for mosaic artists. This chapter is a

very good example of how different people approach the same

subject matter. There are highly realistic birds, such as

Marjorie Knowles' (opposite); naively executed

birds, as in the case of Nicola Haslehurst's

Hen (p.37); Elaine Goodwin's and Jane Muir's

allegorical birds (pp. 30, 31), and humorous birds such as my

Gold-crested Crane (p. 38) or Jeni Stewart–Smith's *Penguins* (above).

⬢ **Swallow** (detail from Taliesin Mosaic pp. 48-49). Martin Cheek.

⬢ **Penguins.** Jeni Stewart-Smith. Vitreous glass, unglazed ceramic and glass roundels.
10 x 20 in (25 x 51 cm). 1997

*In this simple, but beautifully realized mosaic, the comical nature of penguins is
captured. Always be careful not to confuse "simple" with "easy"- it's extremely difficult to
express character with such economy. It is tempting to complicate an image by adding
unnecessary detail, but this will rarely help and is usually the sign of an unsure hand.*

▷ **Wild Birds on West Loch Tarbert** (detail). Marjorie Knowles. Ceramic. Overall
size: 5 ½ x 12 ft (168 x 365 cm). 1990
*The combination of careful observation and meticulous care has created this wonderfully
"realistic" work. Notice how the artist always ensures that there is sufficient tonal
contrast between the subject and background, allowing it to stand out, as, for example,
with the highlighted line that runs along the back of the dominant goose.*

Fountain Mural. Elaine M. Goodwin. Ceramic, silver, vitreous glass, tiles and found objects. 98 x 79 in (2.5 x 2 m). 1994

Though this fountain is clearly readable as water, the artist has made no attempt at realism, choosing instead to create a symbolic feel which merely adds to the overall harmony of the piece.

Happy Birds. Jane Muir. Glass fusions, marble, gold leaf, vitreous and "antico" mosaic. 36 x 21 in (92 x 54 cm). 1995

Jane Muir says that this work celebrates the happiness of living and working close to nature. A lovely sense of poetic lyricism prevails in this calm, meditative piece: the birds are indeed truly happy. There is a sense of tranquillity, which reminds us of the Garden of Eden before all the trouble started. This artist is a master of the medium of mosaic, making it look easy.

◗ **Birds at a Fountain.**
Raymond Gordon. Vitreous
glass and gold smalti.
20 x 36 in (50 x 90 cm).
1995

*Birds at a drinking
fountain was a favourite
theme for the Romans as
well as the Byzantine
Christians. Here, the
vibrant blue of the birds
sings out against the
restrained, white
background. The way the
birds break free of the
border adds fluidity, as
though they have just
flown into the mosaic.*

▽ **Birds.** Tim Turton and Nick Robertson/Art and Design.
Vitreous glass. 24 x 22 in (60 x 50 cm). 1995

*At first glance, this seems a simple piece, but note the
contrast in curves between the bottom left-hand corner and
the andamento of the two penguins. Breaking the flow
using vertical opus for the blue background behind adds
depth and emphasizes the curves. The head of the heron,
popping in from the left, fills the space, its razor-sharp
beak leading the eye across the mosaic.*

◗ **History of Bowls** (detail)**.** Oliver Budd. Smalti and
glazed ceramic. Overall size: 236 x 79 in (6 x 2 m). 1992

*"One for sorrow, two for joy"
describes perfectly how a single
magpie can look ominous but
two, as seen together here, are
harmonious. The striking
plumage of these birds, with its
contrasting blacks, blues and
whites, gives this piece a strong
graphic quality. Notice how the
vertical opus of the tails stands
out against the horizontal flow
of the water beneath.*

Flamingoes
(detail). Jeni Stewart-Smith. Vitreous glass, stained glass, unglazed ceramic and cable strip. Overall size: 18 x 12 in (45 x 30 cm). 1996

Stained glass can be used in mosaic if you choose opaque glass which doesn't need light to shine through it. Jeni started incorporating stained glass out of necessity, through scarcity of materials, but now continues to do so out of choice.

Wild Birds on West Loch Tarbert (detail). Marjorie Knowles. Ceramic.
Overall size: 5 ½ x 12 ft (168 x 365 cm). 1990

Marjorie Knowles' work looks like that of a classically trained painter working in the medium of mosaic. She specializes in large panoramic murals, which necessitate her hiring the local gymnasium to work out her designs. Obviously, the larger the mosaic, the more room there is for accurate fine detail, which this artist clearly relishes. Even where the palette is fairly limited, as here, she has achieved a real sense of perspective and depth in this vast landscape.

Wild Birds on West Loch Tarbert (detail).

There is a terrific sense of distance in this work which the artist has achieved by subtly softening the colours as they approach the horizon. The opus of the background is calm so as not to interfere with the action of the flying geese and the oyster catchers in the middle distance.

▲ **Wild Birds on West Loch Tarbert**
(detail).

*The horizontal opus regulatum of the
sea calms this busy piece down and allows
the vertical neck of the bird to dominate.
Notice the subtly blending colour changes
of the water.*

BIRDS

Two Doves. Rosalind Wates. Vitreous glass and gold. 7 ½ x 17 ½ in (19 x 44 cm). 1993

This artist's work is calm and reflective. Her mosaics don't have instant impact, but their strength increases as you study them. The meditative feel of this mosaic is helped by limiting the palette to one or two carefully chosen colours.

Happy Hen. Nicola Haslehurst. Unglazed ceramic. 5 ½ in (13 cm) square. 1997

The tear-shaped tesserae that make up the body of this cheerful hen create a "feathery" effect and describe her plumpness in a pleasing way.

Love Birds. Emma Ropner. Vitreous glass and raku-fired tiles. 19 x 10 in (48 x 25 cm). 1995

This was Emma's first mosaic, and the inspiration for the design was taken from a greetings card. The addition of the fishy tiles for a border give the piece an extra lively feel. The multi-coloured reds and oranges of the birds work complementary to the greens and blues of the background.

◁ **Canal Birds.**
Emma Biggs/Mosaic Workshop.
Vitreous glass. 100 x 71 in
(250 x 180 cm). 1995

*There is real enjoyment in the
description of the plumage of
the various species of canal
birds shown here. The
restrained colour palette
enables the tiny highlights of
brighter colours, for example,
the red or yellow of an eye, to
sing out. The water is skilfully
handled and a sense of distance
is created through the subtle
colour changes. Some of the
birds are "cut off" by the edge of
the mosaic, so we really feel
that they have just swam past
this window.*

△ **Dove.** Scan Lyon/Mosaic
Designs. Unglazed ceramic.
6 in (15 cm) square. 1997

*Here, only six colours are used,
yet the overall piece looks
exciting nonetheless. Pleasing
and childlike, this mosaic
reminds me of the splendid
prints of birds in flight made by
Georges Braque towards the end
of his life.*

▶ **Turkey**. Martin Cheek. Vitreous glass.
26 in (66 cm) diameter. 1995

This design was taken straight from a 17th-century Mughal Indian miniature and was made for use as a Christmas card. I experimented with different cutting techniques for the plump breast and for the tail feathers. Making the semi-circular tesserae slot together in layers and fanning the tail feathers out to look natural was no easy task, but it is these two elements that make this piece interesting.

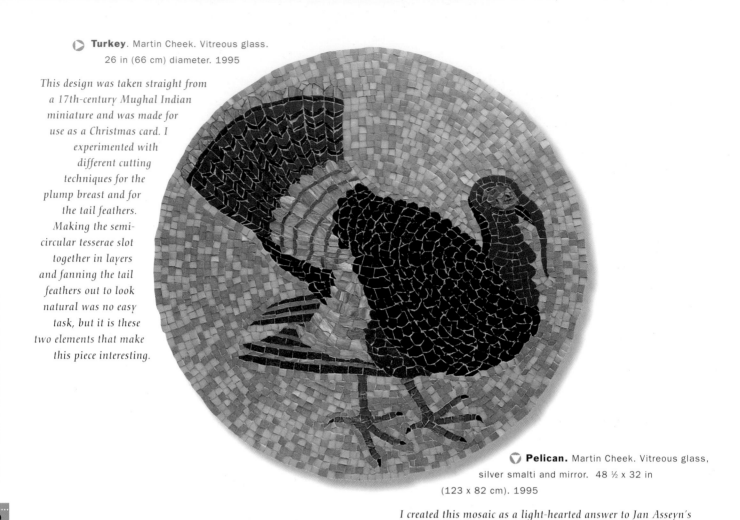

▽ **Pelican.** Martin Cheek. Vitreous glass, silver smalti and mirror. 48 ½ x 32 in (123 x 82 cm). 1995

I created this mosaic as a light-hearted answer to Jan Asseyn's spectacular Threatened Swan in the Rijksmuseum, Amsterdam. The challenge with this piece was in trying to make it simple enough. I liked the idea of the imposing wings coming down on us.

Gold-crested Crane 1.

Martin Cheek. Vitreous glass and gold smalti. 26 in (66 cm) diameter. 1996

These birds seem full of pomp, yet in reality are extremely timid when startled from their posing reverie. The mauve and pink line of the neck has been exaggerated in order to make it stand out sufficiently from the dark purple body. I mosaiced the grass from the nearest blade backwards.

Gold-crested Crane 2.

Martin Cheek. Vitreous glass and gold smalti. 13 ½ in (34 cm) diameter. 1997

I enjoyed working on the crest of the crane above and decided to make another one, this time viewed head-on. The result is unintentionally reminiscent of the haloes seen in the religious icons of the Byzantine period.

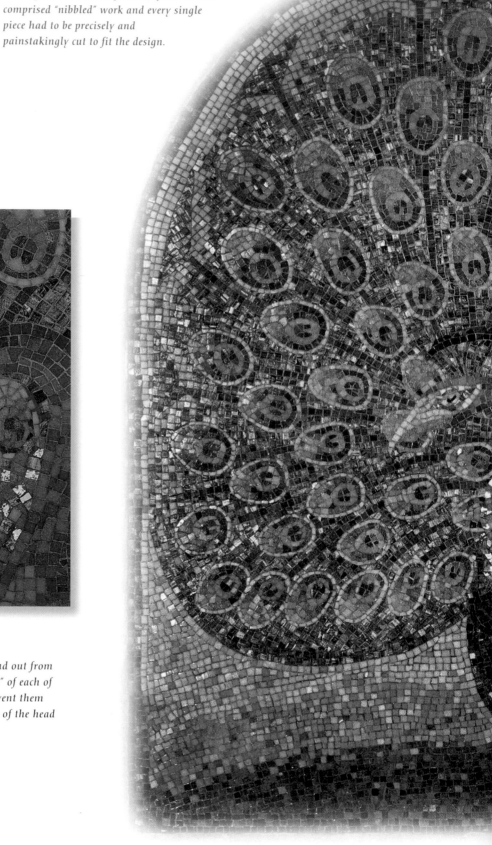

Peacock. Martin Cheek and Susan Goldblatt. Vitreous glass and gold smalti. 55 x 47 in (140 x 120 cm). 1994

This piece, one of a pair commissioned to decorate a wall alongside an indoor swimming pool, took months to complete since three quarters of the mosaic comprised "nibbled" work and every single piece had to be precisely and painstakingly cut to fit the design.

Peacock (detail).

It was quite difficult to make this bird's head stand out from such a busy background, so we arranged the "eyes" of each of the peacock's tail feathers in such a way as to prevent them interfering with its head and neck. The expression of the head seems to capture the conceit of this majestic bird.

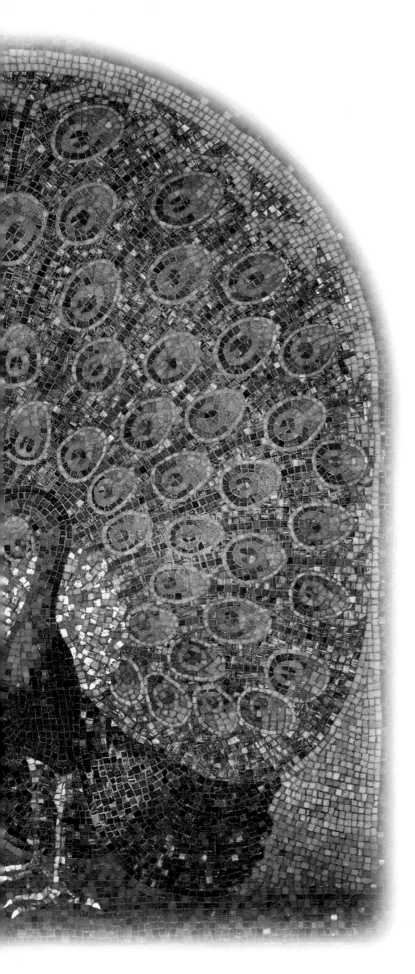

🔺 **Peacock** (detail).

The "eyes" of each tail feather had to be mosaiced in a strict order for them to work effectively. First, the yellow edging was defined as accurately as possible. Then the dark blue 'U' shape was placed in the middle, together with the paler blue outer circle. Finally, the orange and brown surround was filled in. It always helps to decide which is "subject" and which is "background" and to give the "subject" dominance by mosaicing it first. In this case the blue circle was more important than the orange "background". In a similar way the viridian quill was given precedence over the green-veined tesserae behind.

⬟ **Egyptian frieze (1 & 2).** Martin Cheek. Vitreous glass. 18 x 12 in (46 x 30 cm). 1994

I love the directness of Egyptian painting. The birds and animals in particular are a delight and are often masterpieces in pure drawing.
The idea behind these two pieces was gradually to build up panels to make a long frieze of indeterminate length. The hieroglyphics were chosen purely for the way in which they sit within the composition as opposed to having any specific meaning.

◖ ⬟ **Crows (1 & 2).** Martin Cheek. Marble. 18 in (46 cm) square. 1995

A material can often suggest a subject to an artist. I made these birds because I had a quantity of black granite which contains tiny flecks of sparkling mineral and the way they catch the light reminded me of the sheen on a crow's back. The "plain" areas are useful because they allow the subtle changes in the coloured marble to give the mosaics their intrinsic beauty.

Bird. Rajo Taylor-Smith. Ceramic and mirror tiles. 12 ¼ in (31cm) square. 1996

Like Elaine Goodwin, Rajo is an artist who draws her inspiration from India. The influence in this clean, stylish piece is obvious, owing much to the clarity and to the economy of both colour and design also seen in Indian fabrics.

Crane (detail of floor mosaic). Rosalind Wates. Unglazed ceramic. Overall size: 197 in (5 m) square. 1992

A good tip to check if your design will work effectively is to consider the overall shape of the subject in silhouette. Both this crane (part of a kitchen floor mosaic) and the cormorant, below, are clear, uncomplicated shapes. It comes as no surprise, therefore, that the finished mosaics work so well.

Cormorant (detail). Rosalind Wates.

This is a straightforward, but effective mosaic. The background opus *helps to emphasize the bird's pose, while the* opus vermiculatum *is used to create a halo effect and emphasize the flowing lines of the design.*

Celtic Tabletop. Jeni Stewart-Smith.
Vitreous glass. 30 in (76 cm) diameter. 1994

*The three heads cleverly revolve round the
inner circle of this plate. The "negative"
space created by the heads is
reminiscent of a Catherine wheel
and gives the whole piece the
illusion of a revolving disc.*

Hawk (detail). Jeni Stewart-Smith. Vitreous glass.
14 in (36 cm) square. 1984

*Here the artist has abandoned the usual basic
square tesserae in favour of long, thin shards to
depict the feathers of this bird of prey. The
resultant "spikiness" gives the piece an
aggressive edge, reminding us that
this bird is not to be messed with.
Notice how the background is
executed in a similar way to
echo the plumage.*

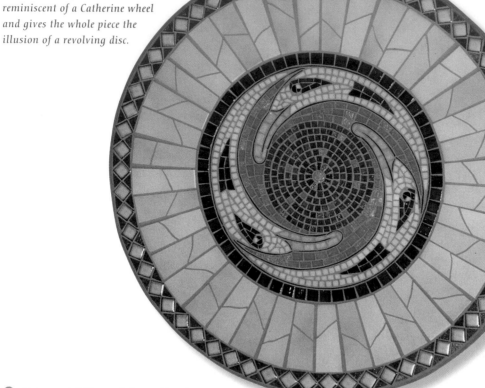

44

Falcon and Discs. Rebecca Newnham.
Vitreous glass, gold and silver leaf. 59 x 39 ½ in
(150 x 100 cm). 1996

*Mosaiced onto a sculpted, three-dimensional form, this Egyptian-
inspired piece has a jewel-like delicacy, but at the same time a
majestic presence, worthy of this aristocratic bird.*

Hoopoe. Emma Biggs/Mosaic Workshop. Marble. 39 x 30 in (100 x 75 cm). 1996

This beautiful mosaic is a prime example of how clarity can be achieved, even within a limited colour range. The inspired use of orange marble for the hoopoe is a perfect choice.

ANIMALS

The beginning of all art was animal art. The animal kingdom

has inspired artists from prehistoric times and this is no less

true of the mosaic artist. The earliest mosaics show

mythological creatures, half man and half beast, as well as the

ever-popular dragons and unicorns.

Mosaic artists may choose animals as inspiration for

different reasons: it may be the appeal of their individual

character, such as Vanessa Benson's elephant (p. 50), or of

their dramatic movement, or it may be because of their striking

markings – see Mosaic Workshop's Moths (p. 55). Whatever the

artist's motive, there is always inspiration to be drawn from

the animal kingdom.

◐ **Siberian Tiger.** Jeni Stewart Smith. Vitreous glass. 12 x 18 in (30 x 45 cm). 1983

Here Jeni has abandoned the familiar square tesserae in favour of acute triangles and diamonds which, she feels, more accurately describe the flow of the tiger's fur. This is a much more tricky and time-consuming option, necessitating exact nibbling of each piece.

▷ **Brazil** (detail). Marjorie Knowles. Mexican glass. Overall size: 10 ½ ft (39 m) square. 1997

There can't be many mosaics of the tapir, a distant relative of the elephant. This vigorous piece, with its unusual view point, is a veritable feast for the eye. The splash of red in the flower on the left lifts the whole piece and makes it seem all the more colourful.

TALIESIN MOSAIC

LAND. I was particularly attracted by the "metamorphosis" sequence, when the witch Ceridwen chases the boy Gwion. He then changes into a hare, so she pursues him in the form of a greyhound; he then transforms himself into a salmon, she into an otter, followed by him changing into a bird and her into a bird of prey. I love trying to put across the individual character of animals in my mosaics, and the challenge of trying to capture three different animals, each having the same personality, was an attractive one.

Taliesin Mosaic. Martin Cheek with Sylvia Bell, Susan Goldblatt, Andrew Higgins, Gary Campbell and the people of Machynlleth, Wales. Vitreous glass and natural stone. Overall dimension of each panel: 94 ½ x 47 in (240 x 120 cm). 1996

This dramatic triptych depicts the popular Welsh legend of Taliesin. The action takes place on land, water and air, so the work was easily divided into three natural panels.

WATER. The effect of the water trailing off the salmon and the otter in this middle panel was achieved by combining broken mirror with silver smalti, used both ways up, the reverse being a lovely, vivid blue glass.

AIR. Susan Goldblatt has a very strong sense of the landscape, which she was able to convey in her design for this background. The sense of flight is emphasized by looking down on the valley below as though you, the viewer, are up there with the two protagonists. The buzzard was inspired by Audubon, the wonderful 19th-century American natural history painter. The bird's eye is a piece of ceramic tile which I shaped and then raku-fired.

Indian Elephant. Sylvia Bell. Unglazed ceramic and raku-fired tile. 20 in (50.5 cm) square. 1996

It's important to remember that the same subject can be interpreted in many ways. Here are three very different approaches to the elephant. The intricate pattern of this animal's blanket was raku-fired onto a pre-shaped tile by the artist. The colours in interior designer Jane Churchill's fabric Indian Summer inspired those of this piece.

Elephant. Sean Lyon/Mosaic Designs. Unglazed ceramic. 6 in (15 cm) square. 1997

In sharp contrast to the two elephants above and below, this gay, cheerful piece is purposefully child-like in design.

Baby Elephant. Vanessa Benson. Marble. 6 ¾ x 10 ¼ in (42 x 26 cm). 1990

Vanessa's work is quiet and always beautifully realized. You can tell that this baby elephant was drawn from life, so accurately does she seem to describe its playful, pachyderm nature.

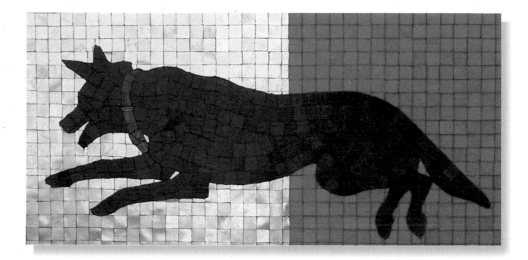

Dog. Rosalind Wates. Vitreous glass and gold leaf. 32 x 21 in (82 x 54 cm). 1991

By simply dividing the background into two halves, Wates has given this piece an intriguing edge - the light background appears much lighter because of the contrast with the "shaded" side.

Greyhounds. Kathleen Stone Sorley. Marble and gold smalti. 16 x 25 in (41 x 64 cm). 1995

This is an interesting study of two sleek canine companions. The restricted palette of coloured marbles undoubtedly gives the piece a strong, graphic quality. The gold smalti for the studs in the dog's collars really shine out in contrast to the more subtle opacity of the natural stone.

Animal Farm Mural. Elaine M. Goodwin and Group 5. Vitreous glass and gold leaf. 32 x 21 in (81 x 53 cm). 1995

These animals are all borrowed from famous traditional Roman mosaics and placed into an exciting new setting. The witty addition of ceramic lids for fruit is inspired. The large "plain" background has been given a good strong texture so as to add interest to these areas, but notice how the opus vermiculatum *is always kept clean and contains no peppering.*

51

ANIMALS

Meditative Toad and Mayfly. Martin Cheek. Smalti and vitreous glass. 47 x 20 in (120 x 51 cm). 1993

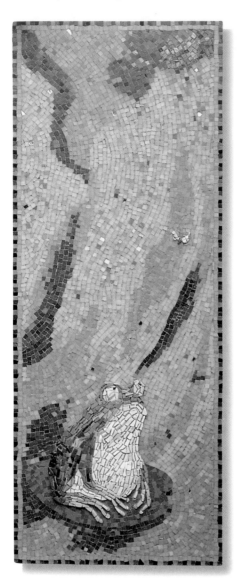

The toad and mayfly are made with smalti, enabling them to stand proud of the vitreous background by ⅜ in (1 cm). I loosely applied a watercolour wash to the backing board which I used as a guide for my mosaic in order to achieve the painterly, airy effect I desired for the background.

Legend of the Wild Boar. Marjorie Knowles. Ceramic. 96 x 60 in (244 x 152 cm). 1989

This piece has been executed almost at life size with a greater degree of realism than any Roman mosaic. Pushing the boar beyond the image and off into the border makes him appear to be actually leaping out of the mosaic. The feeling of distance and of three-dimensional space in this masterpiece is quite astonishing.

The Grizedale Mosaic (detail). Rosalind Wates. Slate, quartz, oxidized stone waste. Overall size: 236 in (6 m) square. 1992

The interesting use of broken tiles with their own individual texture allows the tesserae for this piece to be quite large. The deer appears at first glance to be naively drawn, but closer inspection will reveal how precisely the outline has been described.

The Grizedale Mosaic (detail). Rosalind Wates.

The design for this otter has been reduced down to a carefully observed shape with minimal shading to indicate the form. On a piece such as this, it is most important to create a good, clean, flowing line for the edge of the subject.

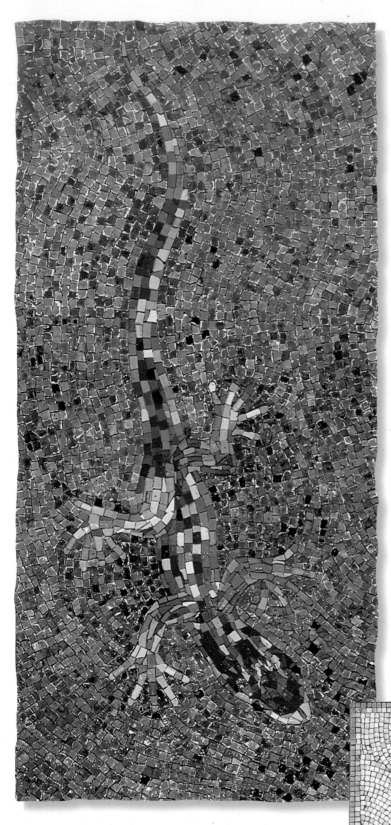

🔺 **Green Gecko.** Martin Cheek. Vitreous glass.
35 ½ x 16 in (90 x 41 cm). 1990

This was one of my first attempts at mosaic. By considering the "line of action" of the lizard and mosaicing the background out from the gecko in this shape, the reversed "S" shape andamento is achieved.

🔺 **Gecko.** Martin Cheek. Smalti and hand-made, raku-fired tiles. 42 x 20 in (107 x 51 cm). 1996

The raku tesserae for the blue background were all fired with the same glaze, but because this process is so infinitely variable, a large variety of subtly different tones can be achieved at once. To make the tesserae, I sculpted a master, from which I made a mould and then slip-cast slabs in white porcelain. The undersides of these slabs were then glazed and broken up into tesserae.

◔ **Moths.**
Emma Biggs/
Mosaic Workshop.
Marble. 29 ½ in
(75 cm) diameter. 1993

*This piece is reminiscent of the decorative
compositions made by the French decorative
artist E.A Seguy in the 1920s.
The monochrome colouring allows us to
concentrate on the pattern and form of the
moths themselves, while the circular format and
the way in which the moths continue beyond the
image give the illusion of looking down through
a microscope at these intricate lepidoptera.*

◔ **Fire Salamander.** Martin Cheek. Marble. 18 in
(46 cm) square. 1995

Another example of opus musivum, *where the line of
action of the main motif continues through into the
background. Although most of this mosaic is made up
of the "plain" background area, the subtle variations in
the natural colours of the marble give it interest.*

LANDSCAPE

The history of mosaic tells a different story from the history of landscape painting. Roman mosaicists often used marble and ceramic for *trompe l'oeil* landscapes which they used to decorate the walls and floors of their great villas, while from the 6th to the 14th century, Andalusia in southern Spain was a Moorish centre for art and culture. The surviving pebble mosaics at the Alhambra in Granada show beautiful, free-flowing floral designs seen alongside the earlier geometric patterns.

▲ **Tree of Life.** Del Palmer. Vitreous glass. 11 ½ x 14 ¼ in (290 x 360 cm). 1995

The ceramic work of Clarice Cliff provided the inspiration for this piece.

▶ **Winter.** Emma Biggs/Mosaic Workshop. Vitreous glass. 39 in (100 cm) square. 1996

Biggs's consummate draughtsmanship is clear in this great mosaic art. I love the subtle, cool, colour range that make this piece so evocative of winter.

 **Golden Sun.** Toby Mason. Coloured mirror. 22 x 6 in (56 x 15 cm). 1996

Though Mason's pieces resemble stained glass, since the light doesn't shine through them but on them, they are, technically mosaics. The tesserae are constructed using traditional mosaic techniques and built up on a foundation of cast cement and unsanded black grout. They are opaque, but appear transparent because of the highly reflective quality of the coloured mirror.

Blue Cloud Sun. Toby Mason. Coloured mirror. 22 x 6 in (56 x 15 cm). 1996

Notice how Mason uses the dark tones around the edge of the composition to lead us into the concentrated light that forms the central focus of the piece.

Purple Sun. Toby Mason. Coloured mirror. 6 x 22 in (15 x 56 cm). 1996

It's interesting to see how close this piece comes to being a totally abstracted picture. There are just a few pointers which enable us to discern the mountains and fields

About Sundown. Toby Mason. Coloured mirror. 6 x 22 in (15 x 56 cm). 1995

Instead of building up a picture in small, square tesserae, here the artist uses large areas of precisely cut pieces to create this glorious landscape. In all these mosaics, the delicate, swirling patina of the coloured glass is allowed to describe the form.

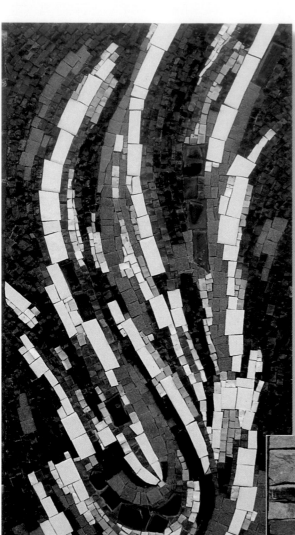

Water Force. Jane Muir. Smalti, tile and handmade glass fusions. 39 ½ x 18 in (100 x 45 cm). 1979

Jane Muir says that her vision concentrates on abstract qualities derived from Nature, with a particular interest in structure, texture, colour and reflected light. She concentrates on Nature itself, as opposed to any specific landscape, and this was a private commission on the theme of water movement. The andamento in this piece echoes free-flowing water.

For and Against (maquette). Jane Muir. Slate, smalti, and weldon stone. 29 x 22 in (74 x 56 cm). 1980

Commissioned by a university, the artist's brief for this piece was to make a mosaic on the theme of academic debate. Muir tries to look deeper, below the surface, in an attempt to bring out the inner meaning of the landscape. The various textures in this piece create a tactile relief and the raised levels of the slate circle create a shadow design which add a three-dimensional quality to the work.

◀ **Gwynedd.** Jane Muir.
Green slate, smalti, gold
leaf and handmade glass
fusions. 12 x 36 in
(31 x 92 cm). 1979

*Muir works in a free way,
assembling the various
elements until she is
satisfied with the result.
This piece focuses on the
landscape formations of
Wales in Snowdonia.
Close examination of the
indigenous moss cushions
were an influence in this
example. Muir has
studied the various local elements closely and then stepped back to
create a piece reminiscent of an aerial view of the landscape.*

▶ **Fruiting.** Jane Muir. Smalti
and handmade glass fusions.
12 in (30 cm) square. 1994

*There is an interesting tension
between the matt, non-
reflective hard slate and
natural stone and the
brilliance of the highly
reflective smalti in this
piece inspired by the theme
of an orchard.*

61

LANDSCAPE

Tree of Life: With Hope One Can Dance Without Music.
Elaine M. Goodwin. Marble, smalti, antique gold and mirror. 39 ½ in
(100 cm) square. 1996

*Inspired by a Japanese proverb, from which it takes its name, the tree of life is
used here to interpret this timeless saying. The tree is a recurring theme in Elaine
Goodwin's work, which she uses to symbolize her personal spiritual message.*

Sand Dunes. Clare-Marie Hill. Ceramic tiles. 56 x 35 ½ in (142 x 90 cm). 1994

A vista of rolling sand dunes, slowly sculpted by wind and time, forms this landscape. Instead of the usual, definite lines of flowing, regular tesserae, in this piece each area is treated as another area of "crazy paving". Because the tonal range is strong and the colours have been carefully chosen, the overall effect is very striking.

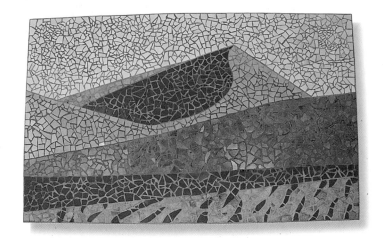

Aerial View. Tessa Hunkin/Mosaic Workshop. Vitreous glass. 180 in (450 cm) square. 1993

This piece has a patchwork quilt quality to it and was based on memories of the sea, shore and the coastal strip of fields and trees.

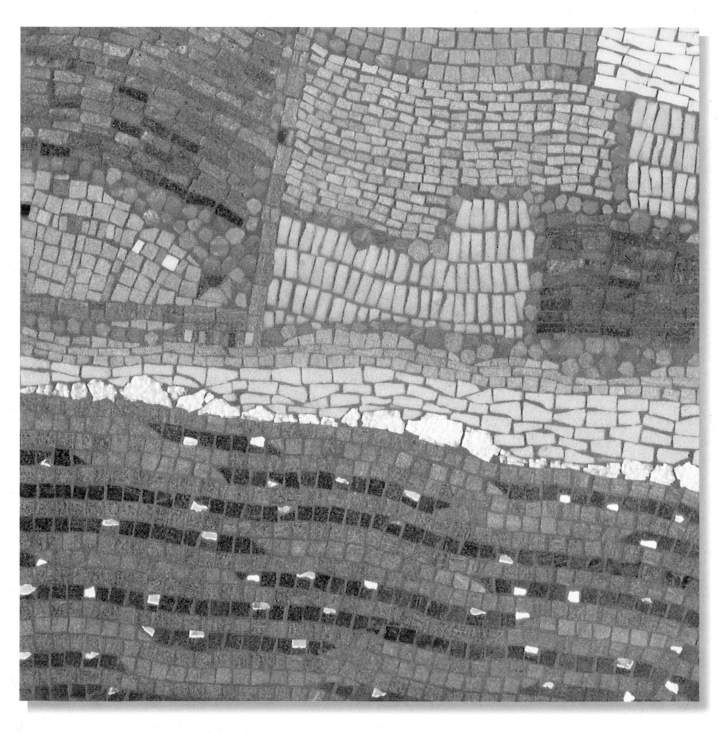

▶ **Florist's Shop.**
Oliver Budd. Smalti and cut
tiles. 18 ft 6 in x 10 ft 8 in
(555 x 321 cm). 1990

*Here we can delight in
recognizing the different flowers
in this feast of bright colour, in
much the same way that we can
in a real flower shop. This piece
was commissioned to brighten
up a dark, oppressive subway.*

◀ **Convolvulus.**
Nick Robertson/Tim
Turton/Art & Design.
Vitreous glass.
11 x 15 in (28 x 38 cm).
1996

*I love the simplicity of
this delightful piece. The colours are cheerful and clear, standing out well
against the dark background. The addition of the blue tesserae within the
white petals emphasizes their whiteness.*

▼ **Trees.** Vanessa Benson. Marble
and unglazed ceramic. 79 x 27 ½ in
(200 x 70 cm). 1995

*This mosaic was inspired by medieval
botanical drawings. Benson says that
her images emerge from the unlocking of
patterns and marks made while
breaking the stone.*

Water Lily.
Vanessa Benson. Smalti and marble. 12 x 7 in (30 x 18 cm). 1996

The artist was commissioned to portray this endangered species of lily. Because of its very brief, two-day, flowering time, Benson had to use historical botanical drawings for reference. Smalti, with its subtle variation of bright and pastel colours, is the ideal medium for this delicate and sensitive piece.

Daisies. Del Palmer. Vitreous glass. 19 in (48 cm) diameter. 1996

One of three mosaics from a series of decorative paving slabs made for a flower garden.

Iris. Del Palmer. Vitreous glass. 19 in (48 cm) diameter. 1996

Tulips. Del Palmer. Vitreous glass. 19 in (48 cm) diameter. 1996

Sunflower Table. Elizabeth Raybee. Ceramic tiles. 28 in (71 cm) diameter. 1994

The inspiration for this piece came from a cache of tiles left over from a remodelled Art Deco-era apartment building.

THE HUMAN WORLD

THE HUMAN FIGURE HAS dominated the history of mosaic. The Romans loved to show themselves at work and at play. Later, the religious mosaics of the Byzantine period elevated the depiction of the human face to a higher spiritual plane.

The human figure offers the greatest known challenge to any artist, and life drawing continues to be taught in art schools because all the disciplines of proportion, perspective, form, colour and tone are to be found in it.

Stylized Portrait. Trevor Caley. Broken ceramic and terracotta. 28 x 24 in (70 x 60 cm). 1984

A superb example of mosaic realism. When seen from a distance, the subtle skin tones fuse together and create an extremely lifelike image.

Pulcinella. Martin Cheek. Vitreous glass, unglazed ceramic, smalti, mirror, raku-fired tiles. 36 x 54 ½ in (92 x 138 cm). 1993

This is a good example of how mixed media can be used to greatly enhance a piece. Because the unglazed ceramic does not reflect the light, the chequered floor recedes visually, allowing the reflective surface of the other materials to come forward.

◗ Castor and Polypences.
Rebecca Newnham. Glass, gold and silver
leaf. 31 in (80 cm) diameter. 1993

*The mosaic work of Rebecca Newnham is often
very sensual, as in this fine example.*

◐ Virgo. Tessa Hunkin/Mosaic
Workshop. Marble. 6 ft 6 in
(200 cm) diameter. 1995

*There's a lovely fullness to this
figure whose flowing lines dominate the
circular space so well.*

She. Elaine M. Goodwin. Smalti, Carrara marble, antique gold, gold smalti. 41 in (105 cm) square. 1995

This piece is one of a pair, entitled He and She, which was inspired by classical sculpture.

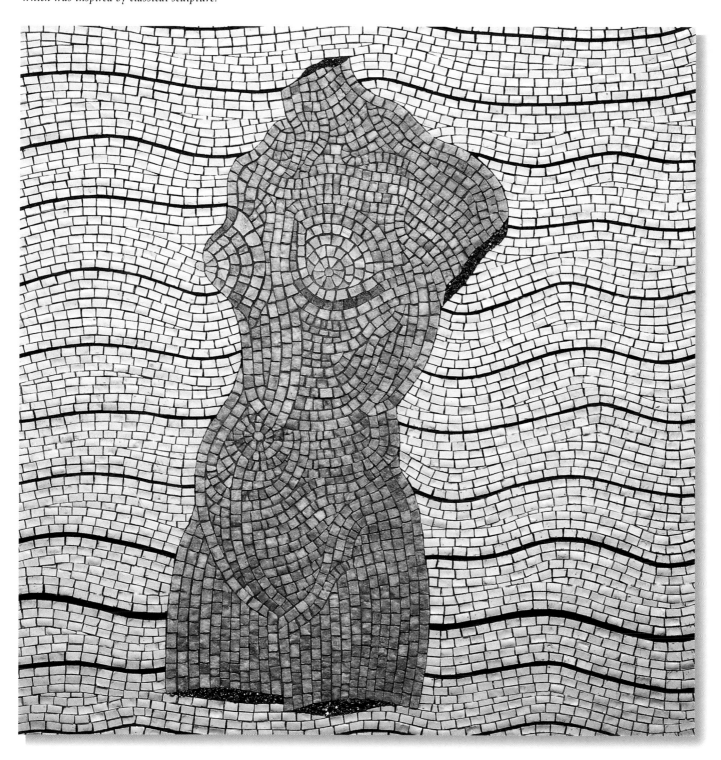

Overleaf: **Prometheus Stealing Fire from Heaven.**
Marjorie Knowles. Ceramic tile. 5 ½ x 12 ft (168 x 365 cm). 1997

This magnificent mosaic hangs on a wall at a fire-fighting equipment makers, so the subject of Prometheus stealing fire from heaven seems entirely appropriate.

⬭ **Progress.** Tessa Hunkin/Mosaic Workshop. Vitreous glass. 30 x 20 ft (900 x 600 cm). 1993.

This allegorical figure looking into the light is unashamedly modern in style, and the choice of colour with the subtle blues and viridian is exquisite. The pattern within the border adds to the regal, stately air.

⬮ **Male Head.** Tessa Hunkin/Mosaic Workshop. Vitreous glass. 11 ft 6in (350 cm) square. 1996

This piece has a wonderful sculptural quality, reminiscent of the huge stone heads carved by sculptor Elizabeth Frink. I love the way that the dark areas are juxtaposed against the light to create strong, vertical bands of tone (emphasized by the vertical opus regulatum) which help to create a tense, laconic mood.

72

◁ **Female Head.** Tessa Hunkin/Mosaic Workshop. Vitreous glass. 11 ft 6 in (350 cm) square. 1996

This lady has an artistic, pensive otherworldliness about her. One feels that this is more than just a picture of a head, but a true portrait which speaks volumes about her ethereal character.

▽ **Four Seasons - Autumn.** Tim Turton/Nick Robertson/Art & Design. Smalti and vitreous glass. 63 ½ x 31 ½ in (160 x 80 cm). 1996

The palette of delicate, autumnal colours is very evocative of the season. Marrows, squashes and pumpkins add a decorative element, the bands of yellow in the two marrows really sing out against the surrounding browns and add depth to the piece. The addition of the human figure, buried behind the fruit and vegetables, emphasizes their abundance.

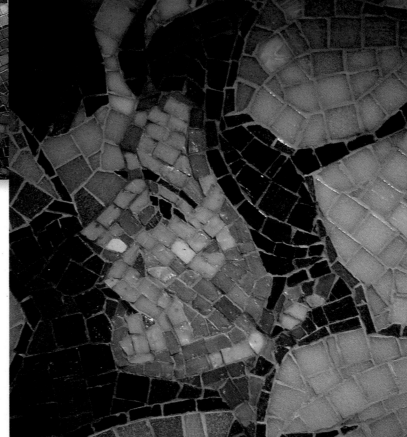

▷ **Four Seasons - Autumn** (detail).
Tim Turton/Nick Robertson.

This fine, beautifully drawn portrait illustrates the range and subtlety that can be achieved by mixing smalti with glass mosaic.

🔺 **Chapel Wall** (detail). Oliver and Kenneth Budd. Smalti and cut tile. 60 sq ft (18.5 sq m). 1989

This piece is one of a series of eight mosaics which depicts the life of a Welsh valley community at around the turn of the century.

Indonesian Figure. Liz Simms. Smalti, gold smalti and mirror. 28 x 19 in (72 x 48.5 cm). 1996

Based on a traditional wall hanging, this piece is also reminiscent of Australian Aboriginal art. It is left to the strong silhouette to describe the form. The subtle variations in the various white smalti add interest, and the gold, although used sparingly, adds a jewel-like quality to the figure.

Happy Washer. Cleo Mussi. Recycled china on enamel bowl. 22 in (56 cm) diameter. 1992

Cleo Mussi's training was originally in textiles and she says that the transition from fabric to china was a natural development. Mussi works in a spontaneous way, allowing the patterned fragments of broken china (mainly accumulated from ceramic dumps) to suggest ideas to her. The result is often humorous and slightly disconcerting.

Before and After School Dinners. Cleo Mussi. Recycled china. 24 x 30 in (60 x 80 cm). 1992

Mussi made this pair of heads as part of a series for a canteen servery. The sense behind the original pattern and design of the individual fragments are taken out of their original context and transformed into unlikely icons, beautiful but at the same time funny and absurd.

Mexican Fountain. Cleo Mussi. Recycled china. 48 x 16 x 16 in (122 x 41 x 41 cm). 1993

Here the artist has developed her earlier work by adding arched panels. The colours are influenced by the architecture of the Yemen. That the piece has an actual function - that of a fountain - adds to its surreal nature.

Punch Flip. Martin Cheek.
Vitreous glass, smalti, raku-fired
tiles. Each panel: 19 ½ x 19 in
(50 x 48 cm). 1993

*My early experience as a puppet
animator is apparent in this
animated sequence. The use of the
raku-fired sculpted pieces helped
with the continuity and to
communicate Punch's mischievous
character. I drew this sequence very
quickly and like the idea of trying
to retain that initial spontaneity,
even though the mosaics took six
weeks to execute.*

◖ **Pierrot, Pulcinella and Harlequin.** Martin
Cheek. Vitreous glass. 50 ½ x 37 ½ in (128 x 95 cm).
1993

*The hoop is something of a gift in that I was able to
radiate out from it to create the spiralling vortex -
indeed the stance of the two outer figures creates a circle
in themselves. Pierrot, the figure on the left, is a good
example of how you build up the figure in "key lines".
The thick border is important here because it breaks the
rhythm and emphasizes the circular andamento of the
piece, just like breaking the rhythm in music.*

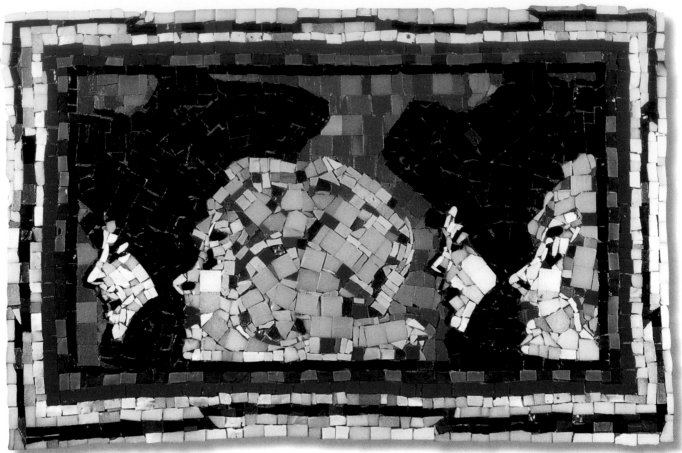

⬆ **Art Nouveau Women #1.**
Greg Kirrish. Marble and vitreous glass.
26 ½ x 18 in (67 x 46 cm). 1996

This image repeats itself, but interestingly, we only need to see the start of the second pair in order to imagine a continuous line of these heads. The flamboyance of Art Nouveau seems particularly appropriate for the medium of mosaic.

⬇ **Prophets.** Tessa Hunkin/Mosaic
Workshop. Smalti. 9 x 16 in (23 x 40 cm).
1996

This mosaic, reminiscent of decorative medieval tapestry or stained glass, has a lovely airy feel to it. There is a strong sense of presence in the figures, even though they are minimally described, have no facial features and stand alone in their spaces.

◯ **Brunel's Bristol** (detail from the Heritage Passage, Bristol). Julian George/Ravenna Arts. Vitreous Glass. Overall size: 21 x 8 ft 2 in (630 x 250 cm). 1994

This mosaic sums up the vast subject of engineering within a single image.

◯ **Cheese Lane Glassworks** (detail from the Heritage Passage, Bristol). Julian George/Ravenna Arts.

This design is clean and to the point. There is a witty comparison between the shapes of the glass vessels and the glassworks chimneys.

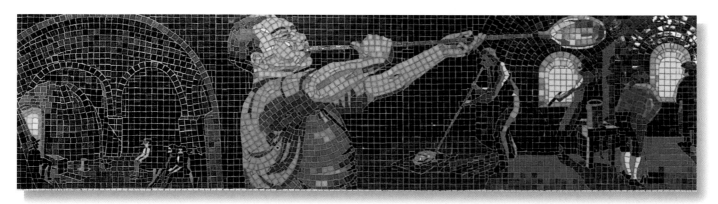

◯ **Blowing Bristol Glassware** (detail from the Heritage Passage, Bristol). Julian George/Ravenna Arts.

The strong, graphic style of this artists is particularly suited to panoramic municipal mosaics designed to cheer up public places. They have the immediate impact of printed posters, but with the added bonus of carefully observed mosaic detail.

Mines Rescue Mural: The Rescue (detail). Oliver Budd. Smalti and cut tile. 22 ft 8 ⅝ x 5 ft 6 ⅛ in (691.5 x 168 cm). 1996

From a mosaic depicting true disaster, this detail shows the point where the rescue team discover the trapped miners. This piece forms part of a triptych whose mood is largely represented by colour. The artist has chosen sodium yellow to symbolize claustrophobia, a red light for danger and bright blue/white light for the relief of having been saved.

Mines Rescue Mural: The Rescue (detail). Oliver Budd

In this detail, the intense feeling of claustrophobia and of actually being trapped is dramatically emphasized.

▶ **Head of an Indian Lady.**
Rajo Taylor-Smith. Vitreous glass,
mirror, stained glass and raku-
fired tile. 8 x 9 in
(21 x 23.5 cm). 1995

*Rajo is a textile designer by
profession who regularly visits
India for ideas and materials.
The design and stylization of
this head is very much
influenced by, and manages to
evoke, the same sense of serenity
that is found in Indian
miniature painting. The use of
the turquoise and white raku tile
for the dress, with its crazed
patina and subtle variation in
colour, is lovely.*

▶ **Roman Bathing Scene** (detail).
Rosalind Wates. Vitreous glass. 59 x 71 in
(150 x 180 cm). 1987

*This piece shows the versatility of Rosalind
Wates's work. There's a lovely feeling of
distance in this piece - one can feel the figure
standing in the space.*

◈ **Indian Woman with Parrot.** Rajo Taylor-Smith.
Unglazed ceramic and mirror. 19 ½ x 26 ½ in (50 x 67 cm).
1997

*A calm, gentle and pleasing mosaic in the soft, earthy colours
characteristic of India. The background is carried out in* opus
musivum, *which gives the piece a lyrical air. The way in
which the peppering of the surround echoes the peppering on
the dress is witty and also helps to unify the overall
composition.*

△ **Somali Woman.** Jo Staniland. Vitreous glass and gold
smalti. 8 x 12 in (21 x 31 cm). 1995

*This piece makes an interesting comparison with the Indian
head, above. The face is very strong and has great dignity
and presence even though it is described quite simply. A sense
of decoration and style are added by the careful use of
gold smalti.*

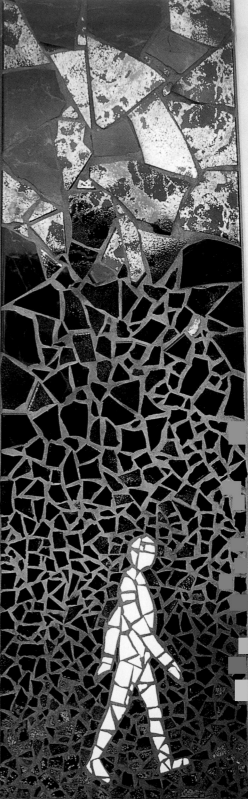

Stan Valler. Trevor Caley. Ceramic. 24 x 28 in (60 x 70 cm). 1989

Although reminiscent of the great portraits to be found in Roman mosaics, there's a wonderful, timeless quality to Trevor Caley's exquisite heads which is all their own.

Underground Numbers 1 & 2. Clare-Marie Hill. Ceramic tile. 12 ½ x 41 in (32 x 104 cm). 1996

The addition of simple human silhouettes lends a sense of proportion to this landscape, without which this would be a piece of natural abstraction. By gradually increasing the size of the tesserae towards the top of the piece, the artist implies a vast space above and beyond the mosaic itself.

Minerva. Marjorie Knowles. Ceramic. Approximately 5 x 3 ft (150 x 90 cm). 1986

Once again, the fine draughtsmanship of this wonderful artist is evident in this striking piece which was made for a carriage on the Orient Express named after the goddess of war and learning. Great skill and painstaking patience are required to create a monochrome mosaic such as this.

Dionysus. Rosalind Wates. Unglazed ceramic. 35 ½ in (90 cm) diameter. 1994

A graphic, contemporary interpretation of the Roman style, this amusing piece is a celebration of the timeless pleasure of drinking wine.

87

ABSTRACT DESIGNS

A BSTRACT ART is non-representational. Sometimes, artists are trying to

capture a specific mood, emotion or feeling. Often, the title of a piece

will give a clue to its meaning, but where a piece is untitled, we

make of it what we will. The captions to the following works are

my personal response to them. Many of the mosaics in this section are purely

decorative and are intended simply to please the eye.

Zigzag Series Panel # 8 (detail).
Lynn Denton. Handmade tile and mosaic.
17 x 26 in (43 x 66 cm). 1990

The brashness of this zigzag design suggests musical overtones, evocative of jazz. This unashamedly loud, celebratory piece was commissioned for a bank.

Atahualpa's Dream. Toby Mason. Glass.
21 x 16 in (53 x 41 cm). 1992

Mason describes this mosaic as "an agate roundel surrounded by a stream of consciousness from the scrapbook." His cites his inspiration as "serendipitous intervention".

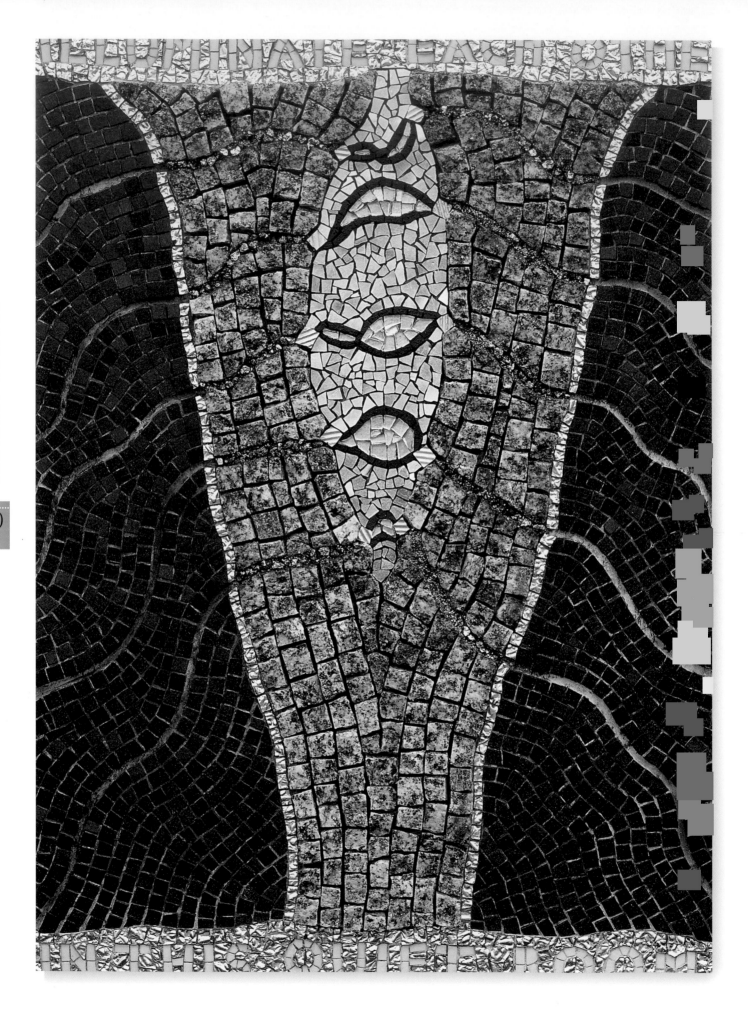

○ **Illuminate Each Other.** Elaine M. Goodwin. Granite, unglazed ceramic, vitreous glass and smalti. 9 ¾ in x 11 ½ in (25 x 29 cm). 1996

An organic tree of life with roots reaching ever outwards was the point of departure for this meditative piece. The title is taken from a haiku by Basho, the Japanese poet.

◁ **Sea Poem I.** Elaine M. Goodwin. granite, antique gold, smalti and "fool's gold". 18 in (45 cm) square. 1996

This piece is one of two works visually inspired by the sea view above St Ives in Cornwall. It is meditative in concept and Goodwin says that she was aiming to explore an icon-like image for contemplation.

Triptych in Yellow with Charles and Di. Cleo Mussi. Recycled china. 4 ft x 5 ft (120 x 150 cm). 1993

Inspired by the architecture of the Yemen and North Africa, this essentially decorative piece pays homage to religious triptychs. The suns are made from crockery made by Ben Su, a ceramicist from Barcelona.

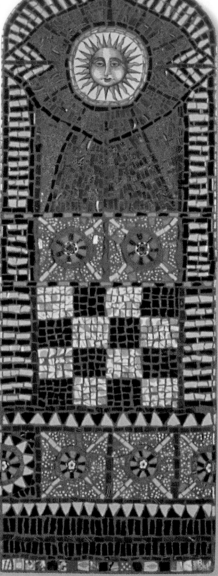

Pool of Colour (detail of table top). Cleo Mussi. Recycled china on Redwood ply. 49 in (125 cm) diameter. 1993

Mussi has a wonderful sense of Mediterranean colour and pattern, which prevails in all of her work. She says that this piece is inspired by Moroccan ceramics. It uses the star as a kind of Islamic motif. There is also a navigational feel to this design.

Double-Axe Foyer (detail). Lynn Denton. Stoneware. 17 x 26 in
(43 x 66 cm). 1986

*The repetition of the Cretan double axe motifs combines to produce this pleasing
mosaic, which has been executed in a sensitive palette of earthy colours.*

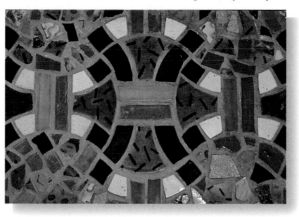

Green Flower Mirror.
Rajo Taylor-Smith. Mirror and
vitreous and stained glass.
12 x 19 in (31 x 49 cm). 1996

*A simple, but effectively decorated
mirror suggesting Arabic and
eastern influences.*

Stars in Stone.
Rajo Taylor-Smith. Unglazed
ceramic and mirror. 12 x 19 in
(31 x 49 cm). 1996

*Islamic architecture and the
constellations inspired this piece.*

ABSTRACT DESIGNS

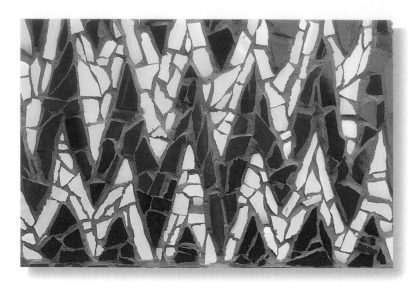

Section of an Arched Panel. Wendy Davison. Glazed ceramic. 7 ¼ x 4 ¼ in (18.5 x 11 cm). 1996

A violent splitting apart or fusing together is suggested in this mosaic which visually recalls electricity or lightning.

Mosaic Matters No. 4. Susan Goldblatt. Vitreous glass. 17 x 12 in (43 x 30.5 cm). 1995

The grid in this design creates a kind of negative space, each square containing a mini icon. One's brain naturally tries logically to link these pieces together, though sometimes images flow through behind the grid and sometimes they do not.

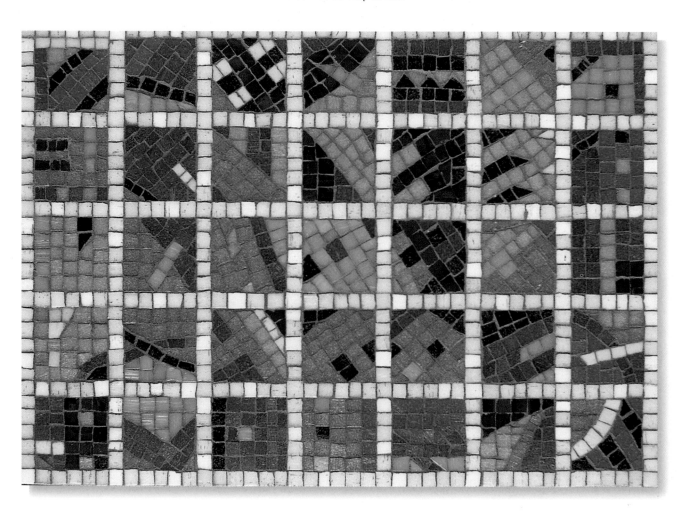

Mirrored Floor Tile.
Rajo Taylor-Smith. Unglazed ceramic
and mirror. 12 in (30 cm) square.
1996

*This piece was inspired by Indian
embroidered textiles. The repetition
of the simple motifs add a certain
lyricism to the overall feel of
this piece.*

Shop Interior. Rebecca Newnham. Vitreous glass and gold leaf,
gilded to glass. 4 ft x 2 ft (120 x 60 cm). 1993

*Created to decorate the side of a desk in a shop, the vivid colours of this
piece add a stylish touch to the whole interior. Rebecca Newnham gilds her
own gold glass, which makes the apparent extravagance of this design
more affordable.*

▶ **Balloon.**
Martin Cheek, Alan Welcome,
Andrew Higgins. Unglazed ceramic,
raku-fired tile.
37 ¾ x 36 in (122 x 90 cm). 1996

*Very obviously a hot air balloon, the disparate images on the
tiles suggest the places, people, animals and the wonders that
you may see as you drift across the sky. This piece was made
from my stock of reject raku tiles.*

▶ **Planet 2.** Emma Biggs/Mosaic
Workshop. Marble. 3 ft 11 in x 24 in
(120 x 60 cm). 1983

*Organic aimless wanderings reminiscent of a
snail trail exist behind lines of longitude focusing
at one point. The shapes created in the lower half of the image
appear to be aiming towards a central point on the elliptical shape
above. The artist tells me she tried to treat the individual tesserae
like stitches in tapestry and play with the idea of distortion.*

Toby Mason. Glass. 16 x 22 in
(41 x 56 cm). 1991

*Mason describes this piece as
"an experiment in
impossibilities inspired by the
engravings of M.C. Escher".
Lines flow in elliptical orbits
which intersect and divide the
space into interesting areas.*

Bathroom Interior
(detail). Steve Melton.
Ceramic and mirror. Overall
size: 6 x 10 ft (180 x 300 cm).
1997

*Melton is very interested in
microbiology and it was his
fascination with cellular
structures that inspired these
two pieces. His knowledge of
figurative sculpture is also
apparent here.*

Bathroom Interior
(detail). Steve Melton.

*In an attempt to explore the
very elaborate "inner
universe" of microbiology,
this piece evokes the
underwater world, with
forms that resemble man-
made industrial piping or
organic worm casts.*

GEOMETRIC BORDERS

Even the simplest border, consisting of a single row of tesserae, will still manage to act as a "frame" for the enclosed mosaic, while large decorative borders can become objects of beauty within themselves. Use isometric or grid paper to work out your own designs.

Chequered strip. Mosaic Workshop. Vitreous glass.

Though only a few rows deep, this simple design can give a wall or floor "weight" around the edge.

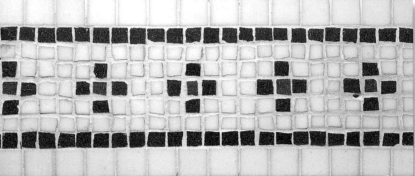

Simple squares. Mosaic Workshop. Vitreous glass.

Another simple pattern comprised of basic square tesserae. It is also possible to put together such designs using uncut tiles.

Six squares. Mosaic Workshop. Vitreous glass.

Positive and negative colours (purple and green in this case) produce a lively effect when alternated. The fact that both colours contain blue gives this border harmony.

U-turns. Mosaic Workshop. Vitreous glass.

A simple design, easy to execute, which nonetheless produces a dramatic effect. It reads the same when viewed from top or bottom.

Eight squares. Mosaic Workshop. Vitreous glass.
A completely different effect to the six squares border is achieved by simply adding an extra tessera at the top and bottom of the squares. Notice how this seven-tesserae-wide strip can be converted to a five-wide strip by turning the motif by 90 degrees.

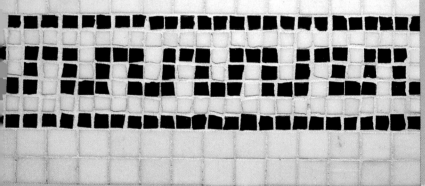

Trellis. Steve Charles. Ceramic.

This latticed grid can be easily constructed on squared paper and adapted to suit your needs.

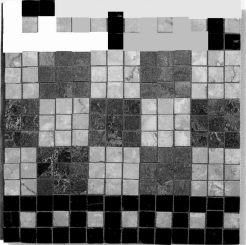

Multi-squares. Mosaic Workshop. Ceramic.

This design can be expanded or reduced to fit any area. Notice how, though fewer in number, the pale beige teserae on the top and bottom strips stand out much more than the black ones.

▷ **Inverted 'T'.** Steve Charles. Ceramic.

This border is very common in Roman mosaics. The beauty of its simplicity is that it looks exactly the same when viewed from upside down, a great benefit when set into a huge floor space.

◁ **Meander**. Steve Charles. Ceramic.

The border pattern at the top is a version of a "fret" or Greek key pattern. It works particularly well on large floors.

▷ **Zigzag.** Mosaic Workshop. Vitreous glass.

This zigzag looks very loud when executed in stark black and white, but the striking pattern can be toned down by selecting two tonally similar colours.

◁ **Diamonds.** Mosaic Workshop. Vitreous glass.

This design requires careful nibbling if it is to look neat. The vertical connecting tesserae should be perfectly straight and parallel to their neighbours.

▷ **Corners.** Mosaic Workshop. Ceramic.

With basic patterns, turning a corner in mosaic is straightforward. Ensure that all the corners work as a whole - this may mean having opposite colours at each end, like, for example, a chessboard, or finishing each row with the same colour (e.g. black). If the tesserae don't fit exactly, you have the choice of spacing them all out evenly or working from both ends to finish with odd tesserae in the middle.

WAVES, KNOTS & FLORAL BORDERS

Waves and knots make an excellent choice for borders for large areas of flooring and there are many styles to choose from. Remember that borders don't always have to be repeat patterns. With "natural" subjects such as plants and flowers, so long as one line (e.g. a plant stem) is continuous, the surrounding motifs (e.g. leaves and berries) can be placed almost at random without spoiling the unity of the piece.

⬤ **Waves I.** Mosaic Workshop. Vitreous glass.

This design is quick to execute, requiring basic, square tesserae for the crests, which are mosaiced first. The rest of the wave is then "filled in" with opus regulatum.

⬤ **Waves II.** Steve Charles. Ceramic.

This wave border uses only a single row of tesserae to describe the wave itself.

⬤ **Waves III.** Steve Charles. Ceramic.

There are many patterns which give an illusion of three dimensions. Here the effect is achieved by "shading" in the areas created by the wavy line.

⬤ **Waves IV.** Martin Cheek. Vitreous glass.

In this pattern, which is quite precise, each tessera has been carefully nibbled to describe the crest. The remainder of the wave has been executed with opus musivum.

⬤ **Guilloche I.** Steve Charles. Vitreous glass.

The classical guilloche design has two or more bands twisting over each other. This can be adapted to make a circular border.

⬤ **Guilloche II.** Mosaic Workshop. Ceramic.

Another two-stranded version of this design. Often, you will find three or even four curved strands plaited together in this way.

Mixed motifs. Steve Charles. Ceramic.

For some borders, botanical accuracy is far less important than the harmony created by repeating a stylized motif.

3-D Curves. Steve Charles. Ceramic.

A three-dimensional feel is given to this border by carefully blending the browns through to cream tesserae. It is easy to see how this border would help to relate the whole mosaic to the topography of the surrounding space.

Curved stems. Mosaic Workshop. Vitreous glass.

A good example of how the continuous line of the stem of the plant lends unity to the design, the randomly placed fruits adding colour and interest.

Decorative Panel. Attica. Ceramic.

This design would be particularly suitable as a border for a floral design.

Geometric border. Attica. Ceramic.

The geometric stylization shown here is specially effective when repeated around a large floor or wall, the larger area the more it repeats and the more impressive it becomes.

Leafy tendril. Steve Charles. Ceramic.

Leaves, fronds and tendrils can be used to create useful connecting links in a design as well as having decorative value in their own right.

STILL LIFE

STILL LIFE IS DEFINED as a composition of inanimate objects, and it is often said that it constitutes the artist's equivalent of a musician's scales. Artists of all genres have always been drawn to create a still life at one time or another, for there is something about the inherent challenge and discipline that still manages to attract them to it. Most of the artists in this section also have work elsewhere in this book.

Mum's Cup and Saucer. Darvia Walmsley. Vitreous glass and gold smalti. 9 in (23 cm) square. 1995

Darvia is a stained glass artist by profession, as is apparent from the graphic quality of this piece. The different materials and textures of the various elements that make up the picture are all clearly represented - from the crispness of the tablecloth to the delicacy of the bone china cup and saucer.

Shower Room Interior. Emma Biggs/Mosaic Workshop. Vitreous glass. 14 ft 1 in x 8 ft 2 in (4 x 2.5 m). 1994

As you look at this piece there is a strong feeling of actually being in the room. One can feel the evident enjoyment of having composed and mosaiced all of the various collected elements that make up this composition.

Objects. Rosalind Wates.
Vitreous glass. 73 x 34 ½ in
(185 x 88 cm). 1987

*Although this mosaic includes
studies of two cats, which means
that strictly speaking it should
not be classed as a true still life,
the fact that the cats have been
handled as design elements
within the composition (which
the title backs up) qualifies it for
inclusion in this section.*

Tea Time Table. Clare-Marie Hill. Ceramic tiles, tea
pot, saucers and cups. 37 x 37 x 2 ½ in (95 x 95 x 7 cm).
1996

*The execution of this piece with its chunky elements is
loud and self assured, but the subtle colour range prevents
the overall effect from being brash. It's a disconcerting yet
amusing notion to hang this piece on a wall, since we are
more used to looking down onto a table from above.*

Yellow Interior. Rosalind Wates. Vitreous glass.
76 ½ x 27 ½ in (194 x 70 cm). 1988

*Here is a triptych suggesting a panoramic view broken by
the edges of the panels. I like the way that the chair, vine
and table are cut into, but continue across the break line.
The strong vertical walls at either side help to lead us into
the space beyond. Interestingly, each section still manages
to work on its own. The composition relies heavily on
linking horizontal and vertical lines which create the
harmony and serenity of the piece.*

Argentina Birds. Rosalind Wates. Vitreous glass and gold smalti. 16 ½ x 18 ½ in (42 x 47 cm). 1989

Gold leaf smalti makes these birds sing out against their vitreous background. Notice how one faces away from its companions, breaking the uniformity of the left-hand side of the picture.

108

 **Strawberry Fool, Ratatouille and Carrot Soup.**
Tessa Hunkin/Mosaic Workshop. Vitreous glass.
31 in x 6 ft 7 in (80 x 200 cm). 1996

Together, these panels make up a cheerful and lively mural commissioned specially for the walls of a staff canteen. There is a self-assured simplicity to these designs which belie years of experience on the part of the designer. It can be difficult to use bold colours on such a large scale, and here the neutral grey background is essential in making the design work.

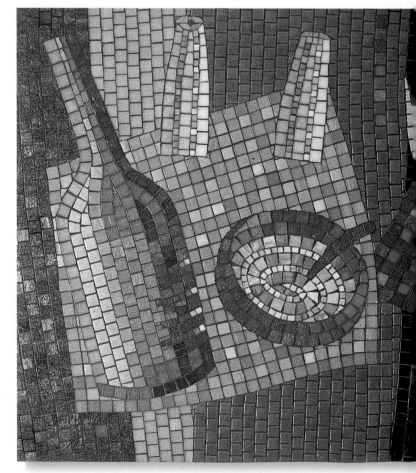

◖ **The Table.** Tessa Hunkin/Mosaic Workshop. Vitreous glass. 31 in x 6 ft 7 in (80 x 200 cm). 1996

The sheer mosaic quality of this entire mural is delightful. For nearly two hundred years (during the 17th and 18th century) mosaic pretended to be painting, aiming for minute realistic detail. These pictures are unashamedly mosaic, each tessera is clearly and graphically visible.

Cooking. Tessa Hunkin/Mosaic Workshop. Vitreous glass. 31 in x 6 ft 7 in (80 x 200 cm). 1993

Here the flames are rendered in cool yellow and blue so as not to distract from the hot red and orange of the prawns.

NATURAL
PEBBLES

ALL OF THE WORK in this chapter is by one artist, Maggy Howarth. Once a painter and

street theatre performance artist, she has since specialized in working with

pebbles and natural stone and, as far as contemporary mosaic is concerned, she

has made the medium her own. No other mosaic artist seems able to achieve the

same clarity and dynamism using this most inflexible of materials.

Bird on Thistle. Slate, limestone, flint and black granite. 4 ft (120 cm) diameter. 1994

This piece was made in two halves, but look how subtly the image is divided: across the tip of the thistle, down the bird's breast, to rejoin the right-hand leaf of the thistle. The focused colour on the body and wing makes sure that it sings out from its surroundings.

Fish (detail). Quartz, granite, glass, limestone. 7 ft 6 in (2m) square. 1995

With its free-flowing lines, this exuberant piece is a masterpiece of pebble mosaic. Carefully selected, rounded, flat top pebbles suggest scales, whilst the fluted fins are carved from ultra-hard limestone slabs which Howarth buys from monumental masons.

⬡ **Chinese Phoenix** (detail). Granite, slate and glass. Overall size: 6 ft (180 cm) diameter. 1995

Here, black "longs", arranged in rows, suggest feathers, whilst the carved green slate used for the beak, the sun's rays and the feather's quill gives additional interest. Notice the cleverly incorporated join line again. It is exactly this clarity, so difficult to achieve in pebble mosaic, which explains why Howarth is considered the master in this field. Spectacular!

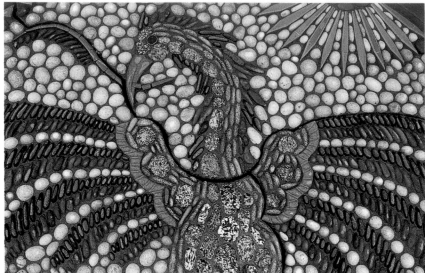

Virgo (detail). Jasper, granite, flint, quartz and slate. Overall size: 4 ft (120 cm) diameter. 1996

Here the bold, white, non-directional "cylinder" stones of the background offer a distinct contrast to the finely worked herringbone on the wings. The subtle variety of greens, greys, browns, reds and ochres is particularly pleasing in this medium.

Capricorn (detail). Flint, granite, slate, quartz and limestone. Overall size: 4 ft (120 cm) diameter. 1996

The concentric circles formed by the stones at the top left draw the eye to their centre, which in turn flows out along the horn of the goat down the side of his head and along his jaw. Curvy, flowing, directional lines create the textural quality of the goat's fleece.

Bull. Granite, jasper, limestone and slate. 39 ½ x 59 in (100 cm x 150 cm). 1994

In order to work in the comfort of her studio rather than outdoors, Howarth has developed an indirect method of construction whereby sections of the mosaic are made in moulds. You can see how this one has been cleverly divided, following the outline of the bull's hind leg. *Notice how the long, white background stones are all set sideways, shooting out from the bull and giving him a fiery, energetic, explosive quality. This effect is achieved by gradually increasing the size of the pebbles in each row as they radiate outwards.*

Heron. Granite, jasper, quartz and slate. 4 ft (120 cm) diameter. 1996

Howarth always lays the stones so as to emphasize the form - look at the way in which the black and grey long stones so perfectly describe the stork's plumage. The strips of stone used for the border, all pointing inwards, focus our gaze on the subject.

Olive Tree. Ceramic, granite, slate and limestone. 39 ½ in (100 cm) square. 1996.

Here, the different types of pebble combine well in describing the knobbliness of the bark. The large, carved stone leaves help to define the shape of the tree and differentiate it from the background. There's a lovely sense of organic growth here, above and below ground level.

▷ **Butterfly.** Flint, quartz, slate and granite. 39 ½ in (100 cm) diameter. 1995

Notice how the brown and white "longs" create flow lines across the wings, crashing through the larger black and white stones used for the markings and giving direction to the basic design.

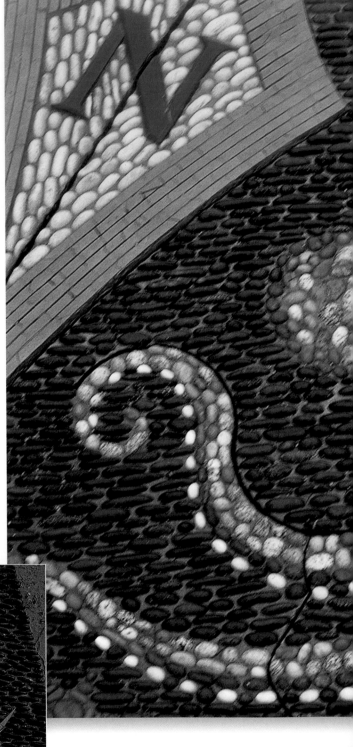

◁ **Mermaid** (detail). Quartz, granite, slate and limestone. 39 ½ x 59 in (100 x 150 cm). 1995

The strips of stone, set on edge, used to describe the hair, also help to break up the surface created by the round "cylinders" and "flat tops". Large white "cylinders" used on the tail have been separated by smaller ones in order to fit them together without gaps. The tail is a single piece of carved limestone.

△ **Octopus.** Granite, flint, quartz and slate. 79 x 39 ½ in (200 x 100 cm). 1997

However complicated the design, Howarth always manages to achieve a strong contrast between the subject and the background - here, light "cylinders" for the octopus are placed against the dark long pebbles of the surround. The pebbles have been graded tonally and by size to accentuate the contours, for example around the back of the head. The long strips used for the compass points break up the uniformity of the areas of round pebbles.

MOSAIC AS SCULPTURE

ONE OF THE GREAT characteristics of

mosaic in the open air is the way changing

light plays on the surface. The placing of these pieces is vitally important – is the

work intended to blend in with or echo its environment? Or is it meant to

dominate the surrounding space? The best results are achieved by commissioning

an artist to make work specifically for the location, as in the case of Rosalind

Wates' mackerel (pages 126–7).

Convex Mirrors. Rebecca Newnham. Hand-fired glass enamel and gold leaf gilded to glass. 20 in (50 cm) diameter domes standing 5 ft 9 in (180 cm) high. 1995

This Egyptian-inspired motif works beautifully on these splendid domed plates. These domes were initially carved in polystyrene, then covered in fibre glass and finally mosaiced.

Lily Star and Star Lily. Rebecca Newnham. Vitreous glass, gold and silver leaf gilded to glass. 6 ft 9 in high x 14 in diameter (200 cm high x 35 cm diameter). 1996

Tired of paying the exorbitant price for gold and silver smalti, Rebecca Newnham has developed a technique of gilding her own glass. These pillars were eventually installed beside the main stairwell of an ocean liner.

Snail and Trail. Martin Cheek. Vitreous glass. 9 x 6 in (23 x 15 cm). 1995

One of a pair of snails racing along my garden wall. Mosaics don't always have to be round or square. When setting this indirect mosaic onto the wall, I rendered a larger area than the snail and then scraped the cement back once the piece was in situ. The mirror was added later using the direct method.

Mole.
Martin Cheek.
Vitreous glass
on steel plate.
18 x 29 in (46
x 74 cm). 1997

This cheeky character was originally designed as a sundial with his nose serving as the "blade" and lots of smaller mounds of earth acting as hour markers. The mole was mosaiced using the indirect method and then fixed onto the steel plate using epoxy wall adhesive.

Leaping Salmon. Martin Cheek. Vitreous glass and mirror on steel. 29 x 20 in (148 x 106 cm). 1997

In the right light, the river water seen through the holes in the mosaic water trail almost merges visually with that reflected in the mosaiced mirror. This piece was made indirect by fixing the glass and mirror tesserae onto a steel plate using an all-purpose, weatherproof epoxy. The trail of water was then added using the direct method.

◗ **Miori.** Steve Melton. Blue ceramic
tile, bronze protusions, mirror tile.
Approximately 5 ft 10 in tall (178 cm).
1995

*This life-size figure looks stunning, set
in the surroundings of the polygonal
courtyard of Boulogne's famous château.
Its considerable size plays an important
part in giving this sculpture its strong,
three-dimensional presence which these
reproductions can only partially convey.*

◖ **Miori** (detail). Steve Melton.

*The form of this figure is sexy and sleek,
but with the addition of incongruous,
knobbly, bulbous protrusions. These were
made by taking a mould from inflated
polythene bags and casting them in
bronze. By profession Melton is in
charge of a bronze-casting foundry at a
college of art and design. An expert at
mould-making and casting, he
incorporates these skills into his mosaic
work to great effect.*

⬥ **Nataweg: Within the Owl and the Woman.** Mireille Lévesque. Slate, calcite, porcelain, vitreous enamel. 48 x 16 in (123 x 40 cm). 1996

Here we have a witty, visual joke with the lady's "bodice" doubling up as the quizzical head of an owl. The natural, earthy colours chosen for this piece work well within its natural setting.

⬥ **Untitled.** Steve Melton. Fibreglass forms, ceramic mosaic and blue glass spheres. 14 ft tall, 6 ½ ft diameter (4.26 m·tall, 1.98 m diameter). 1997

Melton's working method with this type of piece is to sculpt the object in clay and then cover it with fibreglass resin. When the resin has hardened, the sculpture is sawn in half and the clay scooped out. The two halves of the rigid construction can then be resined back together again. The result is a structurally strong, hollow, lightweight shell onto which Melton sets his mosaic tesserae using waterproof tile adhesive.

▷ **Untitled** (detail). Steve Melton.

Melton likes to incorporate protrusions to his sculptural forms, in this case he created hemispheres by sawing blue plastic fishing floats in half and filling them with aluminium foil. There is an otherworldly quality to this piece, made no less unyielding by its huge height.

△ **Mackerel** (detail). Rosalind Wates.

With its rich patterns and wonderful, iridescent colours, the mackerel is an excellent subject for mosaic.

◁ **Mackerel.** Rosalind Wates, Yvonne Murray and the community of North Uist. Pebbles, glass and shells. 16 ft 6 in (5 m). 1996

This prodigious fish looks for all the world as though it has been flung onto the beach by the hand of a careless sea god. A marvellous example of what can be achieved in mosaic, it was made in situ in the Outer Hebrides, where the artist was fortunate in finding a wealth of local pebbles. She also incorporated green and brown glass and blue mussel shells.

This was Wates' first three-dimensional project. The basic structure consisted of an aluminium frame which was bolted to the rock, covered with galvanised mesh, the whole being rendered with a special, sea-water-proof material.

INDEX OF ARTISTS

The artists featured in this book are listed here in alphabetical order. The pages on which their work appears follow each entry. Their work is coded according to the following categories:

P: Public commissions
Pr: Private commissions
R: Restoration work undertaken
C: Courses
K: Kits

Mireille Lévesque

Atelier de La Maison Bleue
22 rue Ste-Anne Varennes
Quebec J3X 1R5, Canada
Fax: 514 652 7563
P; Pr
See p 125

Sean Lyon

Mosaic Designs
14 The Crofts
Stenton
EH42 1TH, UK
Tel: 01368 850 674
P; Pr
See pp 37, 50, 100, 102, 103

Toby Mason

Reflective Glass Mosaics
911 Country Club Drive
Vienna VA 22180-3621, USA
Tel: 703 242 2223
Fax: 703 242 1231
e-mail: masont@erols.com
P; Pr; R
See pp 58, 59, 89, 99

Peter Massey

114 Alfreton Road
Little Eaton
Derby DE21 5DE, UK
Tel: 01332 834 135
P; Pr
See p 12

Steve Melton

Grove Villa
3 Elms Avenue
Ramsgate
Kent CT11 9BW, UK
Tel: 01843 592 197
P; Pr
See pp 98, 122, 123

Mosaic Workshop

Emma Biggs
Tessa Hunkin
Unit B
443–449 Holloway Rd
London N7 6LJ, UK
Tel: 0171 263 2997
P; Pr; R; C; K
See pp 6 (t), 10–11, 12, 14, 15, 23, 37, 45, 55,
56–57, 63, 68, 72, 73, 80, 97, 100, 101, 102, 103,
105, 108–109

Jane Muir

Butcher's Orchard
Weston Turville
Aylesbury
Bucks HP22 5RL, UK
Tel: 0129661 2292
P; Pr
See pp 31, 60, 61

Cleo Mussi

Unit 72C (2nd Floor)
Abbey Business Centre
15–17 Ingate Place
London SW8 3NS, UK
Tel: 0171 498 2727
P; Pr; C
See pp 76, 77, 92

Rebecca Newnham

Kingsgate Workshops
110–116 Kingsgate Road
London NW6 2JG, UK
Tel: 0171 328 6741
P; Pr
See pp 6 (m), 44, 68, 95, 118, 119

Del Palmer

99 Court Road
Eltham
London SE9 5AG, UK
Tel: 0181 859 0128
c/o Novercia Ltd
Tel: 0181 854 9171
Fax: 0181 317 7188
Pr
See pp 56, 65

Catherine Parkinson

6a Dalgarno Gardens
London W10 6HD, UK
Tel: 0181 964 1945
Pr
See p 8

Elizabeth Raybee

ER Mosaics
12773 Pine Avenue
Potter Valley
California 95469, USA
Tel: 707 743 1437
e-mail: raybee@sirius.com
P; Pr
See pp 26, 27, 65

Nick Robertson & Tim Turton

Art & Design
Huntsmoor
Church Lane
Cheltenham
Gloucestershire GL51 5TJ, UK
Tel: 01242 862 444/514 224
P; Pr
See pp 32, 64, 74

Emma Ropner

Hill Top East
Newton Le Willows
Bedale
N. Yorkshire DL8 1TP, UK
Tel: 01677 424 049
Pr
See p 36

Liz Simms

Magpie Mosaics
2 Lambton Court
Bedlington
Northumberland
WE22 5YQ, UK
Tel: 01670 820 360
P; Pr
See pp 20, 21, 76

Alison Slater

114 Alfreton Road
Little Eaton
Derby DE21 5DE, UK
Tel: 01332 834 135
Pr
See p 7 (t)

Jo Staniland

6 Antrobus Road
London W4 5HY, UK
Tel: 0181 747 1189
Pr
See p 84

Jeni Stewart-Smith

24 Carneton Close
Crantock
Newquay
Cornwall TR8 5RY, UK
Tel/Fax: 01637 830 546
Pr
See pp 10, 19, 28, 33, 44, 45, 46

Kathleen Stone Sorley

Low Farthingbank
Dumfries & Galloway
DG3 4EH, UK
Tel: 01848 600 240
Pr
See p 51

Rajo Taylor-Smith

14B Cowley Road
Oxford OX4 1ZH, UK
Tel: 01865 245 253
Pr
See pp 4 (b/r), 43, 84, 93, 95

Darvia Walmsley

Smithy Farm
Cold Row Carrlane
Stalmine
Poulton-le-Fylde
Lancs FY6 9DW, UK
Tel/Fax: 01253 702 531
e-mail: davia@daedalian-glass.co.uk
P; Pr
See pp 5 (t), 104

Rosalind Wates

Malberet
Bar Lane, Owlslick
Princes Risborough
Bucks HP27 9RG, UK
Tel/Fax: 01844 342005
Mobile: 0802 790907
P; Pr
See pp 1, 36, 43, 51, 52, 85, 87, 106, 107, 124, 125

Kim Williams

15 Halliford Road
Sunbury
Middlesex TW16 6DP, UK
Tel: 01932 788553
Pr
See p 7 (b)

GLOSSARY OF MOSAIC TERMS

Andamento The generic word to describe the general "flow" of the mosaic.

Interstices The spaces between tesserae.

Opus musivum See *Opus vermiculatum*.

Opus regulatum A Roman mosaic technique whereby regular, square tesserae are applied in straight rows. The result is like a "brick wall" pattern, often used to fill expanses of background.

Opus sectile When a part of the mosaic, such as a head, consists of a single piece then this part is known as *opus sectile*.

Opus tessellatum Roman mosaic technique using regular, square tesserae to make a rectilinear arrangement. Most frequently used to fill expanses of background.

Opus vermiculatum Roman mosaic technique whereby tesserae are applied in a row around the main motif to create a halo effect and emphasize the setting lines of the design. If the opus vermiculatum is continued outwards to fill a larger area then this area becomes **Opus musivum,** the most rhythmic and lyrical of all the opuses (it literally means "pertaining to the Muses").

Tesserae Roman word meaning cube (pl. tesserae). Tesserae are the basic building blocks of mosaic. The term embraces diverse materials, including marble, ceramic, glass and pebbles.

Acknowledgments and photography credits

The author and publisher would like to thank Clare Maddicott Publications, Cambridge, whose postcard design was the inspiration for the Love Birds on p. 36.

Special photography by Jon Bouchier with the exception of those listed below:

Abacus 21b; Attica 103m/r, b/r; Laura Benson 65t; Vanessa Benson 50b; David Bird 44b, 119; Gareth Blore 62, 90, 91; June Buck/Mosaic Workshop 10-11, 23, 37l, 45b, 68b, 97, 105, 108-109; Kenneth Budd 19b, 64t, 75; Oliver Budd 32b, 82-83; T.J. Caley 66, 86t/l; Martin Cheek 13, 24m, 42t, 54t/r, 120t; Val Corbett 52m/r, b; Johnny Davis 26-27, 65b/r; Lynn Denton 88, 93t; Peter Dobson 8t, 28t, 48-49; FXP 76b/l, 76-77, 92t; David George 100b/l, 101t/r, m/l, 102t/l, m/r, b/r, 103t/r, t/l, b/l; Susan Goldblatt 21t, 94b; Elaine M. Goodwin 30, 51b; Judith A. Gordon 9; Rossman Haigh 36b; Simon Head 64b; Niles E. Helmboldt 51t/l; Mark Holihan 20b; Maggy Howarth 110-117; Jacqui Hurst 52t/l, 54t/l; Paul Kenny 104; Greg Kirrish 80t; Marjorie Knowles 28-29, 34-35; Catherine Leblanc 123t/r; Peter Lofts 87; Evelyn Lothian 46-47; Hazel Lyon 37r, 50m; Derek Magrath 14b; Cristopher Mann 85, 106t, b, 107; Toby Mason 58-59, 89, 99; Paul McConnell 94t; Helen McDonald 125-126; Steve Melton 98, 122-123t/l; John Melville 69; B.J. Middlehurst 81; David Mocatta 61b; Mosaic Workshop 100 except b/l, 101 except t/r, m/l, 102t/r, 103t/l, b/l; Jane Muir 31t/l, 60-61t; Cleo Mussi 77b/l; Susan Olumide 63t, 86r, 106m; Del Palmer 65m/l, m/r, b/l; James Postgate/Mosaic Workshop 12t/l, 14t, m, 15, 55, 57, 63b, 72t, b, 73, 80b; Nick Robertson 32m, 64m; Judy Shapter 32t; Liz Simms 20t, 76t/l; John Stewart-Smith 10, 28m, 33, 44t, 45t, 46; Jens Storch 92b; Mr Supple 53; Michael Taylor 12m/r; Frank Thurston 68t; Tim Turton 74; Rosalind Wates 36t, 43m, b, 51t/r, 87; Shona Wood 50t; Stephen Wright 8m.

First published in 1998 by
New Holland Publishers (UK) Ltd
London • Cape Town
Sydney • Singapore

24 Nutford Place
London W1H 6DQ
United Kingdom

80 McKenzie Street
Cape Town 8001
South Africa

3/2 Aquatic Drive
Frenchs Forest, NSW 2086
Australia

ISBN 1 85368 801 0

Editorial Assistant: Anke Ueberberg
Designer: Grahame Dudley
Special Photography: Jon Bouchier

Editorial Direction: Yvonne McFarlane

Artists on pp 1-7: p 1 Rosalind Wates, p 2 Martin Cheek, p 3 Trevor Caley, p 4 t/r Martin Cheek, m/l Sylvia Bell, b/r Raymond Gordon, b/l Martin Cheek, p 5 t Darvia Walmsley, t/r Maggy Howarth, b Sylvia Bell, p 6 t Tessa Hunkin, m Rebecca Newnham, b Joanna Dewfall, p 7 t Alison Slater, m Martin Cheek, b Kim Williams.

Reproduction by
Modern Age Repro House Ltd, Hong Kong
Printed and bound in Singapore
by Tien Wah Press (Pte) Ltd
2 4 6 8 10 9 7 5 3 1